Willie Mosconi
World's Champion 1941-58

on
Pocket Billiards

CROWN PUBLISHERS, INC.
New York

©, 1948, 1959, BY CROWN PUBLISHERS, INC.

All rights reserved, including the right to reproduce this book, or portions thereof, in any form, except for the inclusion of brief quotations in a review.

PRINTED IN THE UNITED STATES OF AMERICA

Contents

	PAGE
PREFACE	7
1. THE GAME OF BILLIARDS	9
2. FUNDAMENTALS	14

Selection of a Cue – Proper Grip on Cue – Stance at Table

3. THE BRIDGE 22

Hold the Cue Level – Use Short Bridge – Rail Bridge – Stroking Over Object Balls – The Mechanical Bridge

4. STROKE AND FOLLOW-THROUGH 33

Warm-up Stroking – Follow-through

5. CUEING THE BALL 37

Value of Center-Ball – English – Influence of English on Cue Ball – Curve of Cue Ball – Draw and Follow – Elevating Cue – Stop-ball Stroke – Cue Ball and Stroke

6. HITTING THE OBJECT BALL 50

Sighting the Object Ball – Determining Point of Aim – Hitting Point of Aim – Influence of English on Object Ball – Hitting Object Ball on Rail

7.	COMBINATION AND KISS SHOTS.............	60
	Combination Shots — Kiss Shots — Bank Shots	
8.	THE CHAMPIONSHIP GAME (14.1 RACK)....	69
	Opening Break Shot — Safety after Opening Break — Shooting Away — Position Play — Position Play Strategy — Value of Stop Ball	
9.	HOW MUCH DO YOU KNOW?.............	81
	Practice Shots — How to Play Break Shot	
10.	SPEED OF STROKE	98
	Speed and Aim	
11.	PRACTICE AND CONCENTRATION	102
	Concentration — Imagination	
12.	CONCLUSION	105
APPENDIX A.	Glossary of Billiard Terms.......	106
APPENDIX B.	Official Rules — Pocket Billiard Games	115
APPENDIX C.	World Pocket Billiard Champions and Records	142

Willie Mosconi, Pocket Billiard Champion of the World, 1941-1958.

To
My Father
*whose faith in my ability
and whose
encouragement, guidance, and patience
hastened my way
to championship endeavor*

Preface

This book on pocket billiards attempts to cover all phases of the game.

Like a book on any sport, it must apologize to those with some knowledge of the game for the exhaustive discussion of fundamentals.

The organization of the text was planned to take the uninitiated through such elementary steps as the selection of the cue, how to determine the cue's balance, how to make a bridge, and the other basic requirements of good play.

The beginner is urged to follow the instructions step by step as presented, since he must master the phases of play in their proper order to achieve rating as a good player.

We believe, too, that there is much in this book that will be interesting and instructive to men and women who have been playing the game for years.

To the latter, I suggest a study of the Table of Contents for subjects of particular interest, although it is not at all unfitting that even an experienced player review the fundamentals to make sure he has not developed a basic fault of which he is unaware.

WILLIE MOSCONI

1. The Game of Billiards

JUST where and when the game of billiards originated no one knows.

The best historical evidence is that the game originally was an indoor version of lawn bowling, which gained popularity first in England and later in France. This evidence dates the sport back to the fifteenth century.

Shakespeare is responsible for the erroneous belief that the sport was played in the pre-Christian era, since in his *Antony and Cleopatra,* he has Cleopatra say to one of her attendants, "Let us to billiards: come, Charmian." Billiard historians believe Shakespeare winked at the facts. A present-day Shakespeare having Cleopatra present at a baseball game would do no greater violence to fact than did the real Bard in connecting billiards with Cleopatra.

The development of the game of billiards is as vaguely documented as is its origin, but we do know that the Spaniards brought the sport to the American continent in the sixteenth century; that a physician recommended it to Louis XIV of France (1638-1715) as a tonic exercise; that the game was played by George Washington, Thomas Jefferson, Alexander Hamilton, and the Marquis de Lafayette, and that Abraham Lincoln was an ardent cueman.

Billiards became a most popular sport in the United

States in the mid-nineteenth century. Various types of games occupied the players. The first national championship match was played in 1859, the participants being Michael Phelan of New York and John Seereiter of Detroit. The match was played in Detroit with a $15,000 prize. Phelan won and declared himself the national champion.

Championship events in billiards marked the annual sports calendar from 1859 on, but it was not until 1878 that championship play turned to games now popular in the United States. The first world's pocket billiard championship contest was held in 1878, as was the first world's three-cushion billiard tournament. Straight-rail billiards was also a popular carom game, but players became so skillful in this relatively simple game that it gave way in the 1880's to the more difficult balkline games.

With annual championship events, billiards became the national indoor sport after 1878. Meanwhile, the game gained in popularity in other countries. Those familiar with the universal popularity of the game are not surprised by the claim of an eminent sports authority that (prior to World War II) "more people throughout the world play billiards than any other sport, with the exception of basketball."

Down through the years since 1878, the championship games in billiards have been pockets, three-cushion, and balkline. On occasion title events have been held in cushion caroms and red ball. The balkline game, admittedly the most difficult of billiard pastimes, fell victim to the superior skill of Willie Hoppe, Jake Schaefer, Jr., and Welker Cochran in the late 1920's and early 1930's to such an extent that ultimately no other player could compete with them, with the result that world's championship events in this phase of the billiard sport were abandoned after 1935.

Pocket billiards and three-cushion billiards are the only games in which championship events are held today, but the game of snooker, a pocket game of English origin, has been gaining such popularity in the United States that championship events are being planned for this sport.

The name "pocket billiards" is the official designation for the game more popularly known throughout the country as "pool." The game is appropriately named officially, since the players definitely must have a knowledge of billiards to attain a high degree of skill. In pocket billiards, the player, in effect, plays a billiard from an object ball (which he pockets) to a spot on the table, thus getting in good position for his next shot.

Pocket billiards and three-cushion billiards are the billiard games in the United States. While carom billiard games enjoy popularity in metropolitan centers, for the most part, pocket billiards is played in every nook and corner of the country. It would be safe to say that more than 90 per cent of the billiard players in the United States are exponents of the pocket billiard games.*

The game of pocket billiards appeals to men, women, and youngsters of all ages. While it is offered to the general public chiefly in commercial billiard rooms and bowling establishments, nevertheless it always has been a top-ranking sport in church recrea-

---

* Various pocket billiard games are described elsewhere in this book.

tion rooms, on Y.M.C.A. programs, among youngsters in boys' clubs, and in adult clubs of various types.

During the past 25 years, college men and women have been playing billiards in intramural and intercollegiate competition. Until the war interfered, national championships were held for the collegians. After a few years' lapse, the college championships were resumed in the spring of 1947.

During the war officials of the Boys' Clubs of America accepted pocket billiards as a fine competitive sport for the youngsters under their supervision and conducted national tournaments, through a system of keyshots devised by Charles C. Peterson. Club champions of the Boys' Clubs met in national championship play-offs in the spring of 1946 and in each of the following years through 1958.

The war gave billiards great impetus, as hundreds of thousands of enlisted men and women played the game at military and naval training bases. Practically every company dayroom on the army posts had a pocket billiard table for the enjoyment of the soldiers. Tables were also popular recreation facilities in service clubs and in officers' clubs.

The Billiard Congress of America increased the enjoyment of billiards by servicemen and women, sending stars like Peterson, Hoppe, Erwin Rudolph, and Andrew Ponzi into the training camps to teach the sport and demonstrate their cue magic. [EDITOR'S NOTE: Willie Mosconi, a GI during the war, gave exhibitions at posts where he was stationed.]

In the postwar world, the outlook for billiards is better than ever, in the opinion of competent observers. Accepting this fact, the Billiard Congress of

America has inaugurated a program of sectional college tournaments, which will qualify players for the national collegiate championships.

The sectional tournaments are bound to feed the fire of billiard competition throughout the country—and bring forth new players of great skill.

And last, but certainly not least, the Brunswick-Balke-Collender Company, the world's foremost manufacturers of billiard facilities, has opened the door for women to find their way into the billiard sport. For the past few years, Brunswick has been instrumental in planning and outfitting billiard rooms with bowling establishments. These rooms of ultra-modern design offer the billiard sport to all members of the family in a setting which billiards has long deserved. Brunswick billiard rooms in bowling establishments are finding the endorsement of churches, civic officials, and welfare groups.

Within a few years, billiard authorities believe, hundreds of billiard recreation centers patterned after these new combination bowling and billiard establishments will open up in all parts of the country. The response from women who are now enjoying billiards in the plush surroundings of a billiard room in a bowling establishment has been most gratifying and indicative of the appeal the game has to men, women and children alike.

2. Fundamentals

THERE is only one way to play pocket billiards — the right way.

Those who know the right way and apply their knowledge conscientiously can attain a proficiency that will be limited only by the extent of their natural talent. Those who perform the wrong way, either through ignorance or carelessness, will never rise above the level of mediocrity.

The right way in pocket billiards is based generally on a few simple fundamentals. They include:

1. Proper grip on the cue
2. Stance at the table
3. A good bridge
4. Stroke and follow-through
5. Cueing the ball
6. Hitting the object ball

There is more, of course, to pocket billiard playing skill, but unless the player has mastered the above fundamentals to the point where they become a natural part of his game, he never will be much account as a pocket billiard player. Let us consider these fundamentals one by one.

Selection of Cue

When we say "proper grip on the cue" we are referring to the grip of the cue in the right hand. (These lessons assume the player is right-handed. Left-handed players will substitute "left hand," wherever "right hand" is mentioned.) However, before we discuss the grip, let us consider the cue itself. The player should select a well-balanced cue. If the balance is right, the weight of the cue will be distributed evenly. The cue will not be "top-heavy" at the butt end. The proper balance will vary according to the individual player, so experiment with several or more cues until you find the one that is your balance.

The weight of the cue is important also. In pocket billiards, great force is seldom required, so the cue should be of a medium weight, between 18 and 21 ounces. The length of the cue depends again on the individual, but I recommend a cue 57 inches in length for pocket billiards. If the cue is too short, the player will get into trouble when he has to stretch far out on the table to make a shot.

My cue is 57 inches long and weighs 20 ounces. The diameter of the tip is 13 millimeters.

Proper Grip on Cue

After you select a cue which meets your individual requirements, you are ready to consider the proper grip on the cue.

First, you determine the balance point of the cue. You do this by laying the cue across your fingers (Fig. 1) and sliding it along your fingers until the weight of the butt end balances the weight of the shaft. The balance is at the fulcrum point.

Many billiard experts advise gripping the cue at the balance, but I recommend that the cue be gripped

Fig. 1. Proper grip on cue. Determine balance point. Slide cue along fingers until weight of butt end equals weight of shaft.

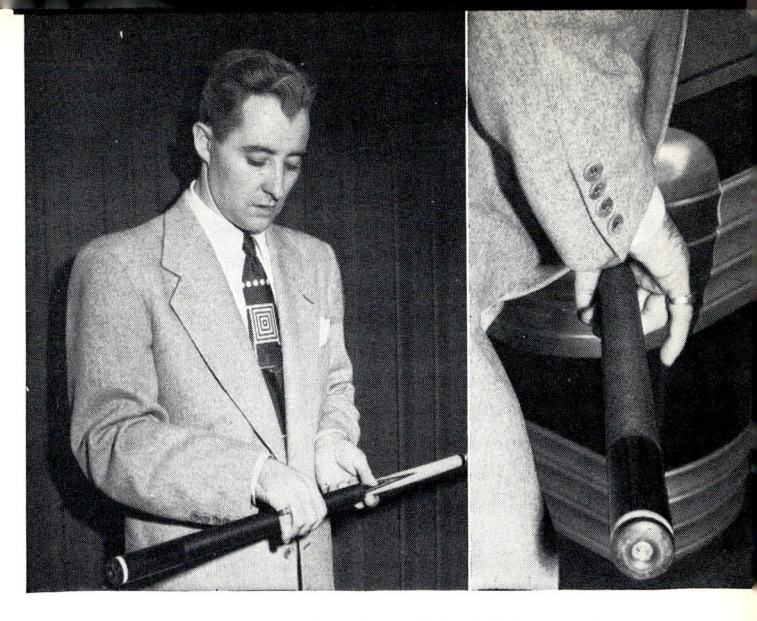

Figs. 2-3. Grip cue three or four inches behind balance point.

three or four inches behind the balance (Fig. 2).

Be careful, however, that you do not grip the cue behind the point I recommend, unless the shot requires a long stretch over the table. If the distance between your bridge hand and your right hand is too long it will tend to throw you off balance.

We now know where to grip the cue with the right hand. The next important factor is gripping the cue correctly. Don't grab the butt end of the cue with a strangle hold. Rather, grip the cue lightly with your thumb and first three fingers. If the cue is gripped properly the butt end of the cue will not touch the palm of your hand. It will rest on your fingers and thumb (Fig. 3).

This light grip on the cue makes for a spring action, which helps impart desired action to the cue ball. A death grip on the butt end of the cue tends to deaden the action of the ball. In addition, the right hand, tightly wrapped about the cue, is likely to become cramped and tired, with a resultant impairment of stroke.

Remember, grip the cue lightly between the thumb and the first three fingers. To get an idea of what I mean, pick up a coffee cup by the handle as though you were going to drink the coffee.

Stance at the Table

No two players stand exactly the same at the table. Good players, however, have these factors in common: They are balanced and comfortable, and their heads are over the cue in the line of aim.

Generally, a player may assume the proper stance at the table by following this formula:

Take your position at the table facing in the direction of your shot. Stand back from the table about one foot. Your right foot is in line with the cue ball (Fig. 4).

Now, turn your left foot about 30 degrees to the right. Move your right foot back until the toe of your right shoe is opposite the middle of your left shoe. The right foot is pointed at a 45-degree angle from your original position. If your position is proper, you can, while standing erect, swing your right arm freely in a line with the cue ball and object ball.

Now, bend forward at the hips. Your weight is distributed evenly on both feet (Fig. 5). In this position, your body can move slightly forward with the stroke. This forward movement will help you follow through on your stroke. Your left arm is ex-

Fig. 4. Correct stance at table. Face in direction of your shot, about one foot back from table, right foot in line with cue ball.

Fig. 5. Bend forward at hips with weight evenly set on both feet. This inclined position will help you follow through on your stroke.

Fig. 6. The body faces the shot, and is balanced to move forward with the stroke. Head is directly above the cue, in line of aim.

Fig. 7. If you must stretch out on the table, take same position. Proper position and balance are the essentials for billiard skill.

ended straight to the bridge position. The left elbow is bent very slightly if at all.

This position is recommended for the average shot on the table. If, for example, the cue ball is frozen to, or is close to, the rail, your position varies. In this case, you would be farther back from the table, but, again, your body faces the shot, you are balanced to move forward with the stroke and *your head is over the cue in the line of aim* (Fig. 6).

If the shot requires that you stretch far out on the table you must also take the same relative position. Your head is over the cue in the line of aim and you move forward with the stroke.

Remember, that proper position at the table is most essential. Proper position is proper balance — and without proper balance, you'll never achieve billiard skill (Fig. 7).

3. The Bridge

DURING a championship game of pocket billiards a player may use various kinds of bridges, depending upon the shot he is shooting, but regardless of the bridge the player uses, the bridge hand must be firm and solid and the shaft of the cue must be held tightly enough so that the flesh of the thumb and fingers moves like agitated jello as the player does his warm-up stroking.

To make a proper bridge, make a fist with your left hand. Now open up your thumb and index finger so they form a "V" or an "L." Lay the cue shaft on the thumb joint where the thumb joins the hand. Now wrap the index finger tightly over the cue shaft. Close the thumb across the first joint of the index finger (Fig. 8). If your bridge is sufficiently tight it will support the weight of the cue as you hold the cue in the air.

Now, with the index finger and thumb still wrapped snugly about the cue shaft, extend your middle, ring, and little fingers (Fig. 9). Now, place the heel of the hand firmly on the table. If your bridge is right, your middle, ring, and little fingers and the heel of your hand will rest solidly on the table (Figs. 10 and 11).

This is the "orthodox" bridge and is to be used on all shots within easy reach and in which the bridge hand can be placed on the bed of the table.

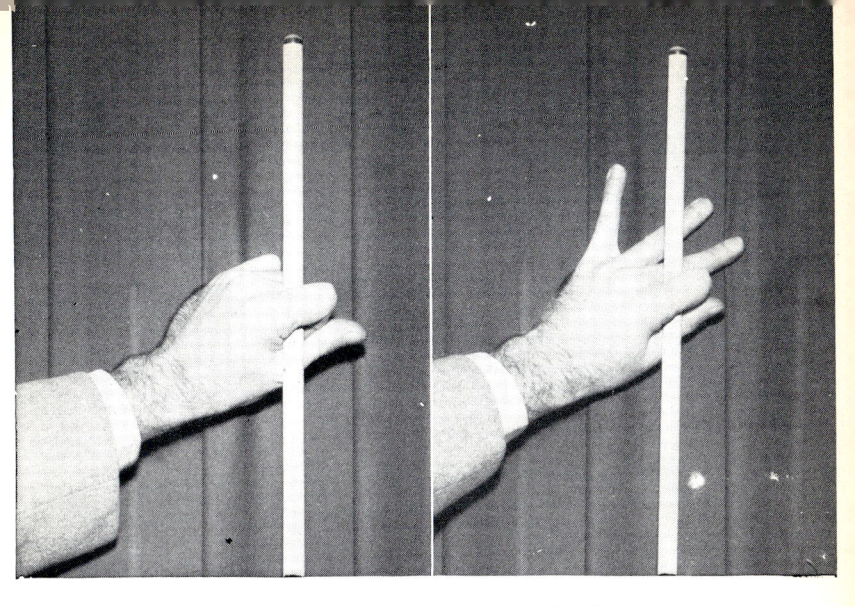

Figs. 8-9. The bridge. Make a fist with left hand. Place cue between your thumb and index finger with the latter over shaft.

Hold the Cue Level

This bridge can be raised or lowered as required for draw or follow shots (Figs. 12 and 13). At this time, it will be well to point out that the cue is held as level as possible on all shots, the bridge hand being lowered for draw shots and raised for follow shots. On a draw shot don't make the mistake of elevating the butt end of the cue and striking down on the cue ball, unless the cue ball is close to the rail or unless you have to stroke over an object ball close to the cue ball.

Situations will arise during the pocket billiard game which will require that you use a different type of bridge, but *remember, always, the bridge should be as firm and tight as is consistent with freedom of move-*

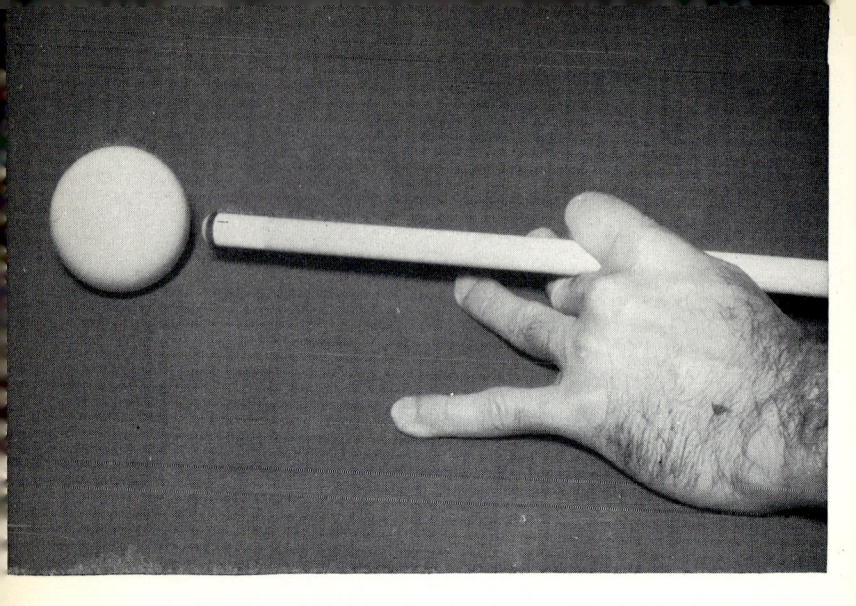

Fig. 10. If your bridge is right, other fingers and heel of hand are on table with index finger and thumb wrapped around cue shaft.

Fig. 11. This is orthodox bridge to be used on all shots within easy reach and where bridge hand can be put on bed of the table.

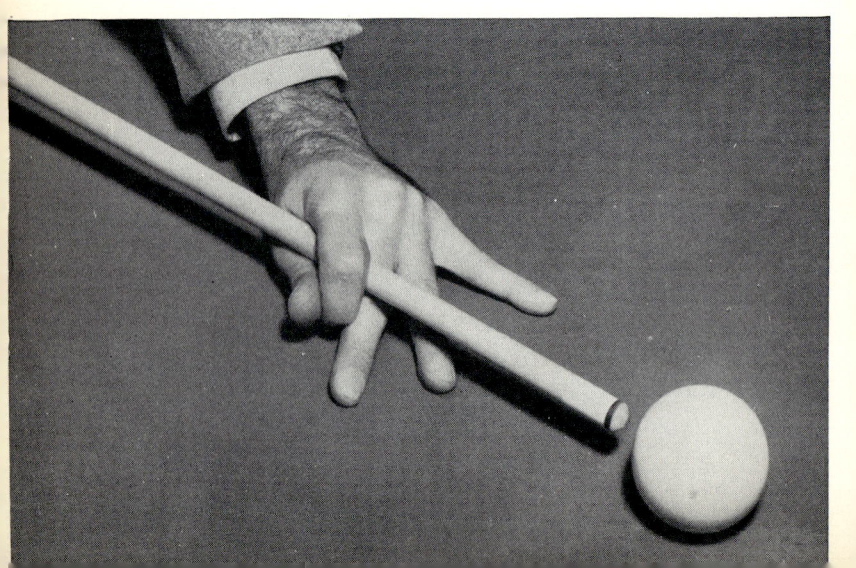

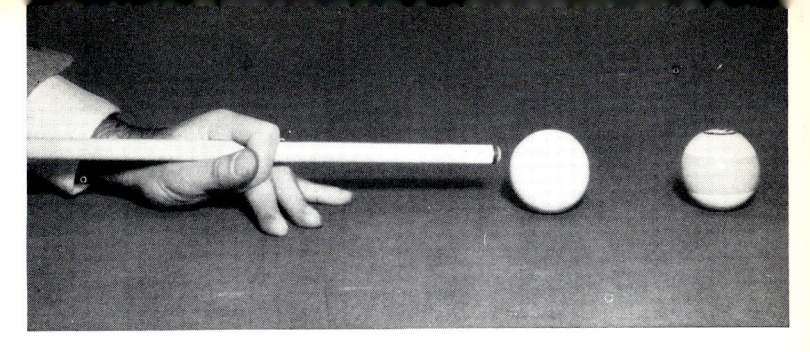

Fig. 12. In raising bridge for follow shots, raise hand, not cue.

ment. Unless it is, the shaft of the cue may sway enough from side to side or up and down to spoil your contact on the cue ball and your aim on the object ball.

Use Short Bridge

It is important, too, that the distance between the tip of your cue and your bridge hand be comparatively short. Never allow this distance to exceed eight inches unless you have to stretch far to reach the shot. The shorter the bridge, the better your control of your stroke (Fig. 14).

If you have to stretch far across the table to make a shot, the bridge will be longer, and whenever possible your thumb and finger should be wrapped around the

Fig. 13. Lower bridge for draw shots. Keep bridge firm and tight.

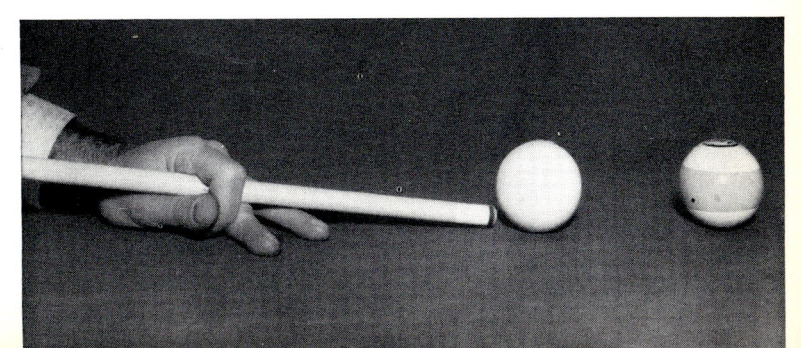

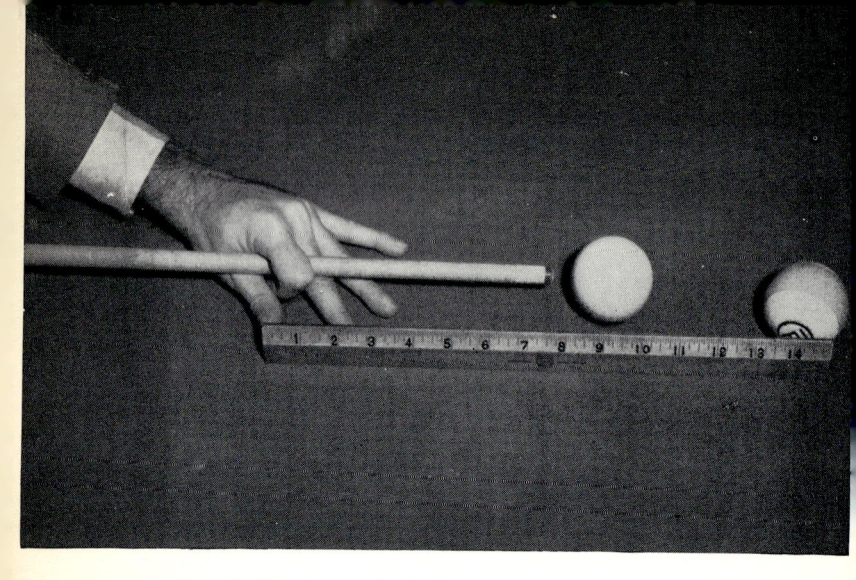

Fig. 14. The shorter the bridge, the better your stroke control.

Fig. 15. A long stretch. Slide cue over "V" of thumb and hand.

Fig. 16. Cue ball near rail. Use this bridge with a firm grip.

cue in the orthodox bridge. However, if the stretch is too long for the "orthodox grip," you can slide the cue across the "V" of your thumb and hand, but make sure again that the bridge is as snug as possible and firm (Fig. 15).

Use of the orthodox bridge is not possible, of course, when the cue ball is frozen to the rail or within eight inches of the rail (assuming you are shooting at a right angle to the rail).

Rail Bridge

When the cue ball is near to the rail, you should use the bridge as illustrated in Fig. 16. The fingers are

Fig. 17. Another rail bridge. Note how fingers are over cushion.

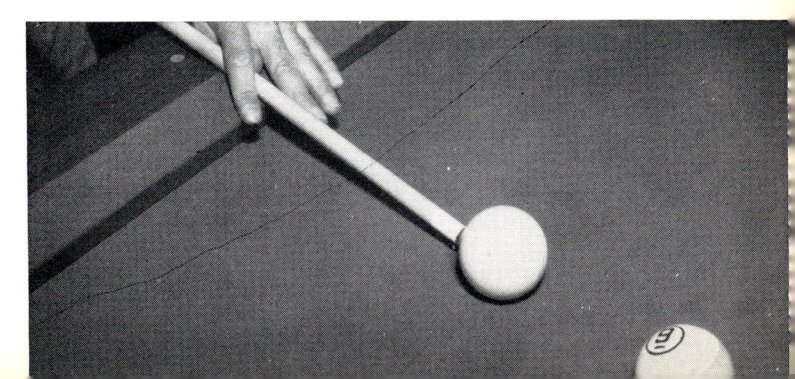

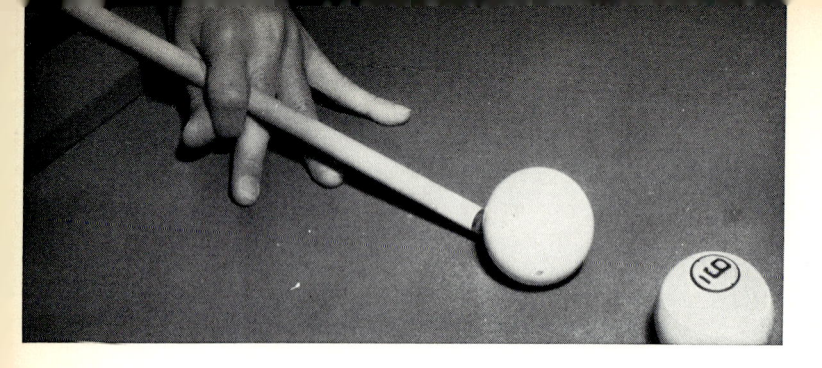

Fig. 18. A bridge on the bed of the table is more accurate than a rail bridge if there is room between the ball and the cushion.

laid flat on the rail, and the cue slides between the index and middle fingers. The middle finger acts as the guide. The fingers are pressed snugly against the cue shaft to assure accurate aim. The thumb, underneath the cue, is also pressed against the cue shaft, serving as a brace and guide. Grip the cue near the balance.

Be careful, while cueing a ball against the rail, that you do not elevate the cue more than is absolutely necessary.

When the cue ball is resting near the rail, but still not far enough away to allow for a bridge on the bed of the table, use the bridge shown in Fig. 17. This is much like the bridge used when the ball is against the rail, except that the fingers of the bridge hand extend over the cushion.

Remember, however, that an orthodox bridge on the bed of the table is always more accurate than a rail bridge if there is room (nine inches or more) between the ball and the cushion (Fig. 18).

Another type of rail bridge is illustrated in Fig. 19. This bridge is used when the cue ball is near the rail and the player is shooting along the rail. In situa-

MOSCONI ON POCKET BILLIARDS

tions such as this, a player may become careless and shoot with a faulty bridge. Always make certain that your bridge is secure enough for accurate aim before you attempt a shot along the rail. Experiment, if you must, with several bridges, until you find the surest one.

Stroking Over Object Balls

About the only other bridge a player will have to use is the one employed while stroking over object balls (Figs. 20, 21). The pocket player must perfect this type of bridge and use it with confidence, because he will be confronted with many situations which require stroking over one or several object balls.

Notice (in Fig. 20) that the fingers are placed so

Fig. 19. For a shot along the rail, choose the bridge that will give you accurate aim. Make sure your bridge is secure enough.

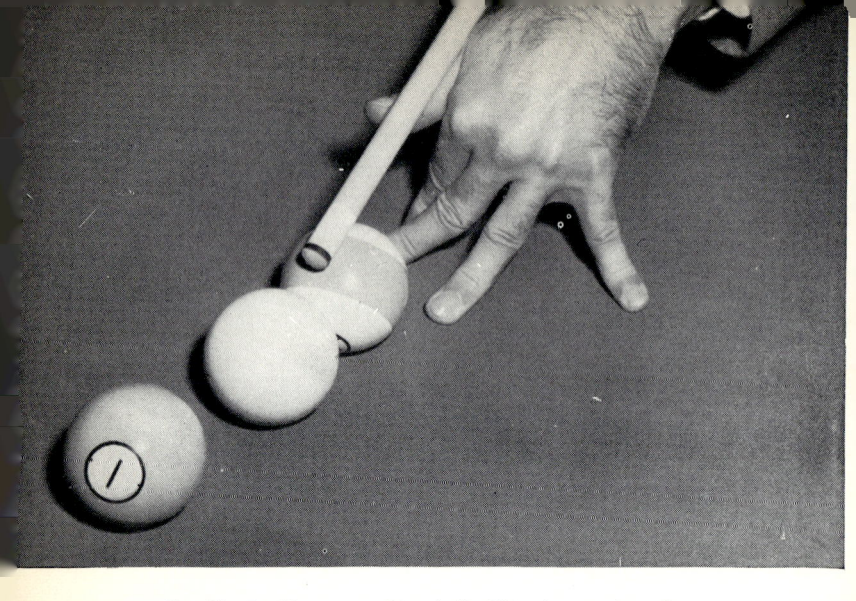

Fig. 20. Stroking over object ball. This shot needs a firm type of bridge. Note how contorted the fingers appear on the table.

Fig. 21. Work on this type of bridge. You will need it often. Fingers must be firmly on the table or the cue will wobble.

Fig. 22. Use the mechanical bridge if you cannot reach your shot. Grip the cue lightly, but left hand guiding bridge must be steady.

firmly on the table that they actually appear contorted. The player needs a solid bridge foundation, more so here than at any other time, since the cue, sliding on the thumb, will wobble if the bridge falters.

The Mechanical Bridge

Many times during the course of a pocket billiard game the player will be forced to use the mechanical bridge on shots that he cannot otherwise reach. Since this is so, accurate use of this bridge is most essential. The first thing a player must remember when using the mechanical bridge is to be most careful that he does not disturb the cue ball or object balls as he places the bridge on the table. If he does, he is committing a foul.

The proper use of the mechanical bridge is illustrated in Fig. 22. Note that the distance from the cue ball is comparatively short to allow for accuracy, but is still long enough to permit smooth stroking. Note the grip on the butt end of the cue. This is the accepted method of gripping the cue. It is substantially the same grip as on a regular stroke.

The left hand, holding and guiding the mechanical bridge, must be steady to assure a secure bridge. Note how the bridge handle is placed firmly on the table. Practice with the mechanical bridge until you can employ it with absolute confidence. Keep the stroke smooth and deliberate, and follow through. If the stroke becomes jerky, you are likely to slide the cue from the bridge, with a resultant miscue or scratch.

On occasion you will have to stand the mechanical bridge on its side to shoot over several object balls. You can appreciate the extra care needed to assure a solid base when using this bridge.

Be quick to use the bridge if you are confronted with a shot that you cannot conveniently reach without the mechanical aid. Don't risk a miss with a sloppy effort, trying to stab at a shot out of reach.

4. *Stroke and Follow-through*

UP to this point, we have discussed the selection of a cue, the stance at the table, the proper grip on the cue, and the various types of bridges. Now we come to the fundamental that can make or break a player — the stroke. Many players have a natural stroke, while others never acquire what might be termed a consistent stroke.

The proper stroke in billiards depends on gripping the cue correctly — that is, lightly but firmly in the right hand. It depends, too, on a good bridge. Also the player's position at the table must be balanced and comfortable. *His head must be over the cue in the line of aim.*

If the player stands right at the table and grips the cue slightly behind the balance, his right arm, flexed at the elbow, will swing in a graceful arc (Fig. 23). The wrist joint will be loose, too, if the cue is gripped lightly in the fingers. This loose action is not possible in the wrist if the player has a death grip on the butt end of the cue.

As the player strokes, swinging his arm back and forth in a pendulum arc, the shoulder, elbow, and wrist joints come into free and easy action. The right arm swings close to the body.

Fig. 23. Position at the table must be balanced and comfortable. For proper stroke, your head must be over cue in the line of aim.

Warm-up Stroking

As the player addresses the shot, with his bridge hand firmly fixed on the table, he should resort to warm-up stroking before he strikes the cue ball. This warm-up stroking grooves the stroke while the player studies the aim on the object ball and the point he must strike on the cue ball. I find that three or four warm-up strokes are sufficient, but some other championship-flight players, particularly those who use a definite pendulum stroke, take as many as a dozen quick warm-up strokes.

These warm-up strokes should be rhythmic; and when the player feels that his stroke is grooved, he shoots at the cue ball. It would be better, perhaps, to say that the player shoots *through* rather than *at* the cue ball, because if he has followed through on his stroke, *as he must,* the tip of the cue will follow through the area occupied by the cue ball before it was struck with the cue tip (Figs. 24, 25).

Follow-through

Without that all-important follow-through, a player will never have a good stroke. A follow-through on the billiard stroke is just as important as a follow-through with a golf club, a baseball bat, a bowling ball, or when kicking a field goal. In billiards, the follow-through imparts desired action to the cue ball. It is most important in pocket billiards, since "desired action" is paramount if the cueman expects to master position play.

By comparing Fig. 23 with Fig. 5, you will note that the player is in the same relative position at the backward and forward points of his stroke. At the backward point of the stroke the hand points down to the floor at approximately a right angle. At the forward point in the stroke, the shoulder is in about the same position; the elbow has dropped slightly, and the wrist moves forward. The cue is held as level as possible.

In Fig. 24 a shot is shown as the player is about to stroke the cue ball. Fig. 25 shows the completed stroke. The cue ball has struck the object ball. The cue shaft has followed through the area formerly occupied by the cue ball.

It is difficult to teach a player a good stroke. It is like trying to teach a fellow to be a .300 hitter in major league baseball. Some people develop a good stroke instinctively. Others never acquire one. Any player, in my opinion, can improve his stroke if he follows the instructions given above.

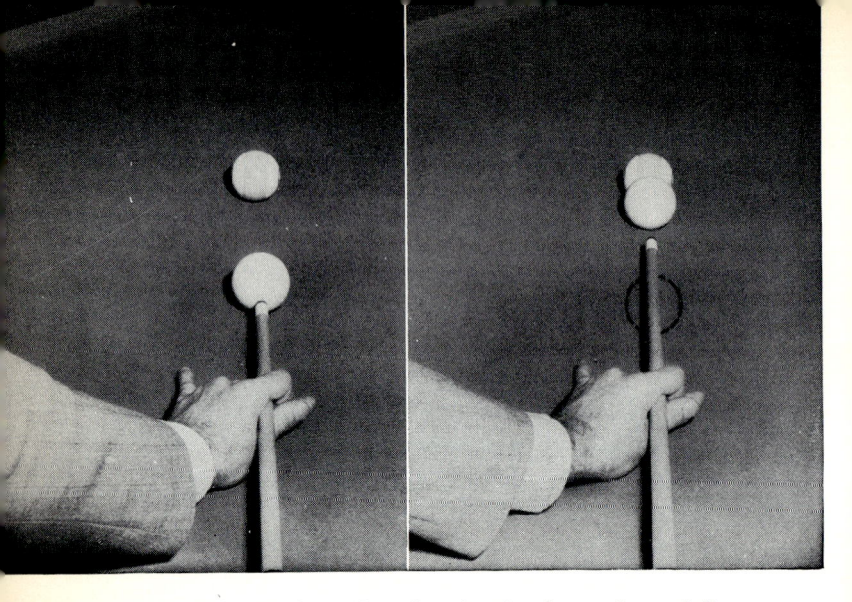

Figs. 24, 25. Stroking. Shoot through rather than at the cue ball. If you follow through, cue tip will go in area cue ball occupied.

Remember, the stroke is not a rigid poke at the cue ball. Rather, it is a springy action. It is accomplished by gripping the cue lightly at the balance. Whiplike action is achieved by a free and easy motion in the wrist, elbow, and shoulder joints. The wrist action gives snap to the stroke. And a deliberate follow-through is most important.

5. Cueing the Ball

THE first essential in the proper cueing of the cue ball is correct chalking of the cue tip. Too many players are careless here — some jabbing the tip of the cue in the chalk and drilling as though they were trying to bore a hole through the chalk. Others keep whirling the cue tip in the chalk while they are studying a shot. Both are bad practices, since they may cake too much chalk unevenly on the tip, to say nothing of causing undue abrasive wear.

Chalking the Cue Tip

The proper way to chalk the cue is illustrated in Fig. 26. The player brushes the cue tip with several light but sure strokes, making certain that he has spread a thin, even coating of chalk on the tip.

The cue tip must be chalked properly — *lightly after every stroke* — to avoid miscues.

Remember, the cue ball is a sphere; it has no flat surfaces. Even when the player hits the cue ball in dead center, he is stroking a round object. The chalk increases the friction between the cue tip and the polished surface of the cue ball. Without this "increased friction," miscues are probable.

Take care in chalking your cue. Remember, an ounce of prevention, here, is worth a pound of cure, if,

Fig. 26. The cue tip must be chalked properly before every stroke. Chalk increases friction between cue tip and the cue-ball surface.

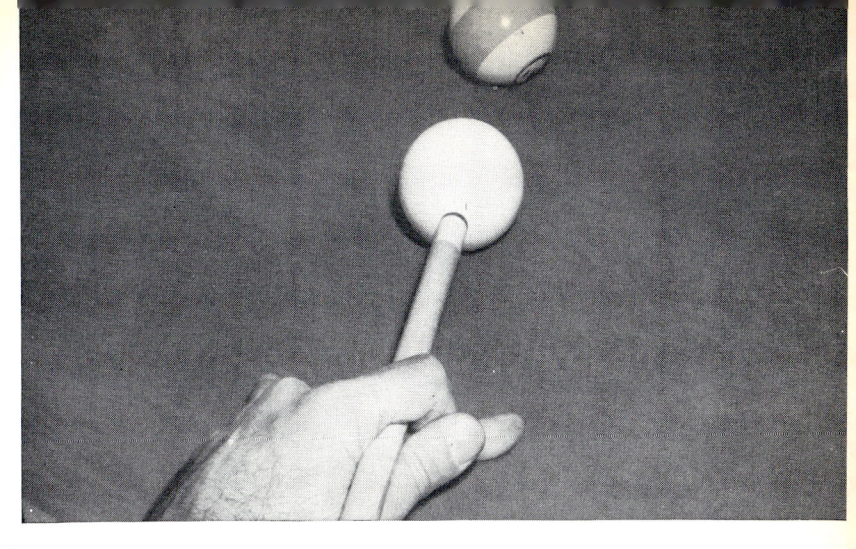

Fig. 27. More than 85 per cent of shots can be made by stroking cue ball in the center. Use center-ball stroke whenever possible.

after a miscue on your part, the opponent runs out the game.

Value of Center-Ball Stroking

Again stressing the fact that the cue ball is round and has no flat surfaces, we cannot overemphasize the value of center-ball stroking. In pocket billiards, my experience has taught me that more than 85 per cent of the shots can be accomplished by stroking the cue ball in the center of its vertical axis.

Fig. 27 shows a center-ball shot. This stroking, as we have pointed out, is recommended for the vast majority of shots. The player will never appreciate just how important center-ball stroking is until he has learned that English influences: (1) The path of the cue ball to the object ball, and (2) the path of the object ball from the cue ball to the pocket.

LITTLE SPORTS LIBRARY

So, unless the player thoroughly understands the influence of English (which we will discuss later), he can miss a shot which he thinks is dead on the pocket.

A good rule to remember in pocket billiards is *use center-ball stroking on every shot* unless English is absolutely required for position or to make a shot that "is not on" without English.

English

We might point out that English is a necessary evil in pocket billiards. Complete mastery of the game depends to some extent on English, but, unless the player understands its application, he can get into more trouble with it than he would without it. Since it has an important place in the game, let us consider its proper application.

English, generally, means spin. If you strike the cue ball to the right of its vertical axis, the cue ball will spin to the left, or counterclockwise along the bed of the table. If you strike the cue ball to the left of its vertical axis, the cue ball travels with a clockwise spin, that is, spinning to the right.

Most billiard authorities insist that all the English necessary for 99 per cent of billiard shots can be applied by striking the cue ball no more than a cue tip-width from the exact center of the ball. Fig. 28 shows English left; Fig. 29 shows English right. My experience in 15 years of world's championship play has convinced me that the "cue-tip-width-from-the-center-of-the-ball" rule is right. If you go to the left or right beyond that point, the danger of miscue increases.

You cannot apply English to the ball in the proper

manner unless your stroke is correct. The cue ball will not take English as you plan it if your stroke is a rigid poke. Rather, your stroke must be springlike; it must be sharp and deliberate, and *you must follow through.*

Influence of English on Cue Ball

English falls into two general categories — natural or running English and reverse English. Natural English will:

1. Add speed to the cue ball after it strikes a cushion.
2. Widen the angle after it strikes a cushion.
3. Throw the object ball to one side or the other from its original course.

Reverse English will accomplish the "reverse" of *1* and *2,* above. It will decrease the speed of the cue ball off the cushion and it will narrow the angle. Reverse English does not apply until the cue ball strikes a cushion.

In other words, if the player decides that he must strike the cue ball with left-hand English to throw the object ball, the English is natural when it strikes the object ball. If the ball goes to the cushion after striking the object ball, in this case the English either remains natural or becomes reverse, depending on the player's intention.

Natural English is applied to the same side of the cue ball that the player wants the cue ball to travel after it strikes the object ball or a cushion. If the player wants the cue ball to travel to the left, he strikes the cue ball to the left of center. If the ball is to go to the right, he strikes it to the right of center.

Reverse English is applied to cause the cue ball to

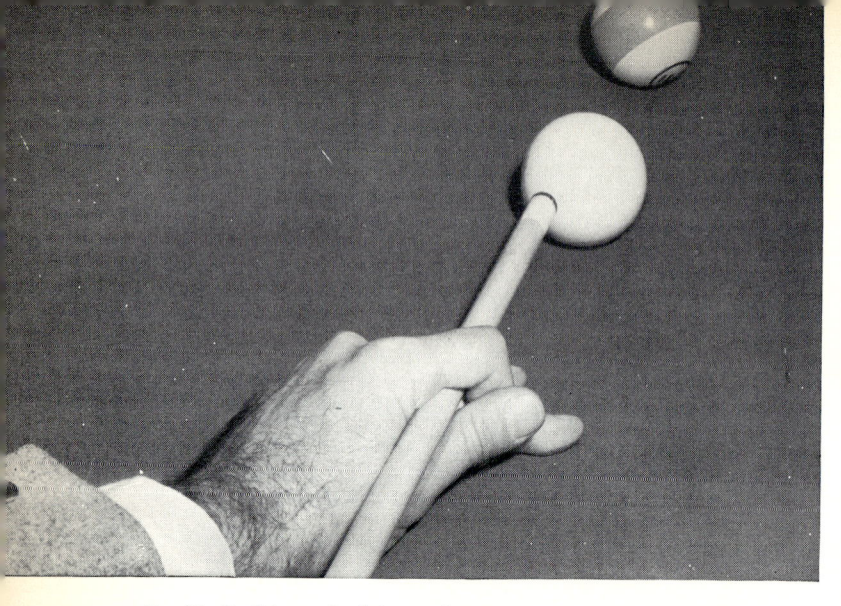

Fig. 28. English to the left. English means spin. If you strike cue ball to left of axis, it will spin to right and curve to left.

Fig. 29. English to the right. Ball will spin to left, curve right. Follow through sharply when applying English to cue ball.

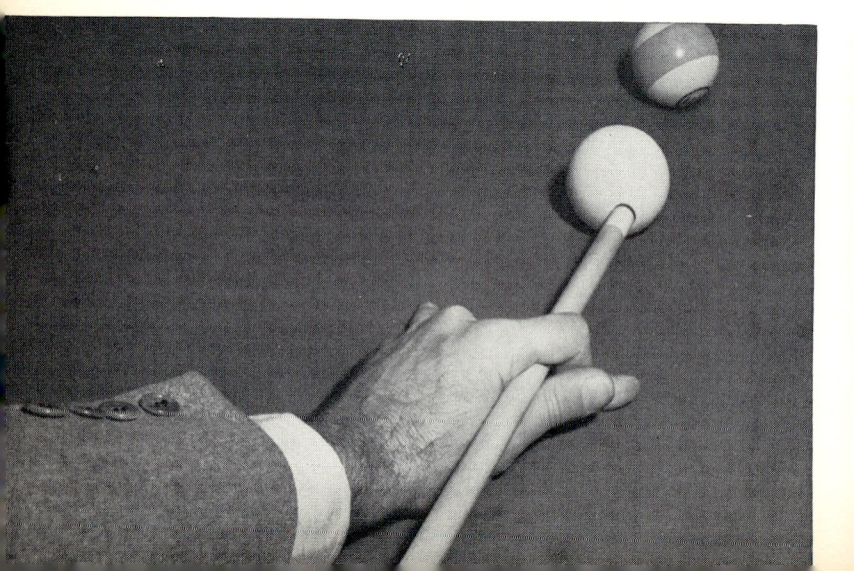

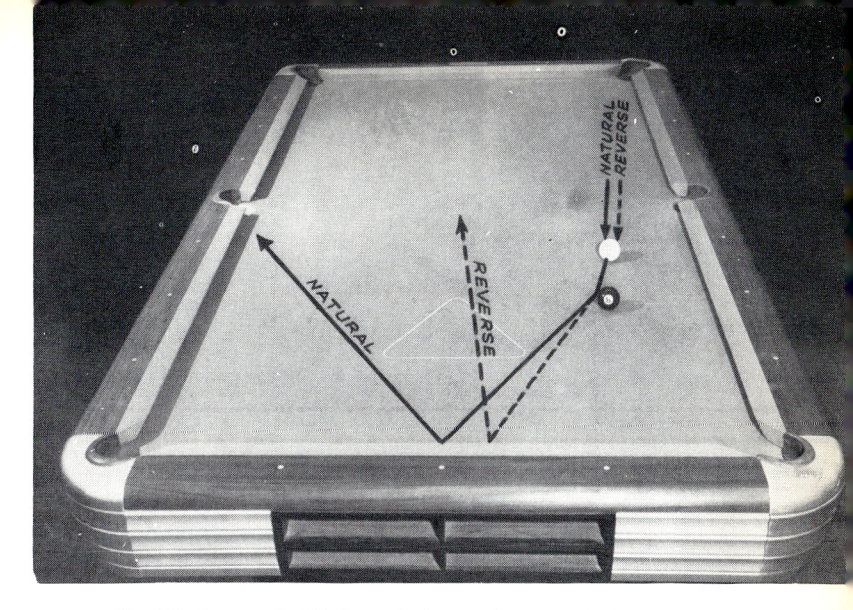

Fig. 30. Reverse English is applied to make a cue ball deviate from the line it would normally travel after hitting the cushion.

"reverse" the course it would normally travel after hitting a cushion (Fig. 30).

Curve of Cue Ball

The player must also understand the *curve* of the cue ball. English will influence the path of the cue ball to the object ball. A cue ball Englished on the right curves to the right as it approaches the object ball. If struck on the left it will curve to the left as it approaches the object ball (Figs. 31, 32).

The radius of the curve is in direct proportion to the length of the shot. Understanding this, the player can adjust his aim on the object ball to accommodate the anticipated curve. When, for example, the player shoots a length-of-the-table shot with English left, he

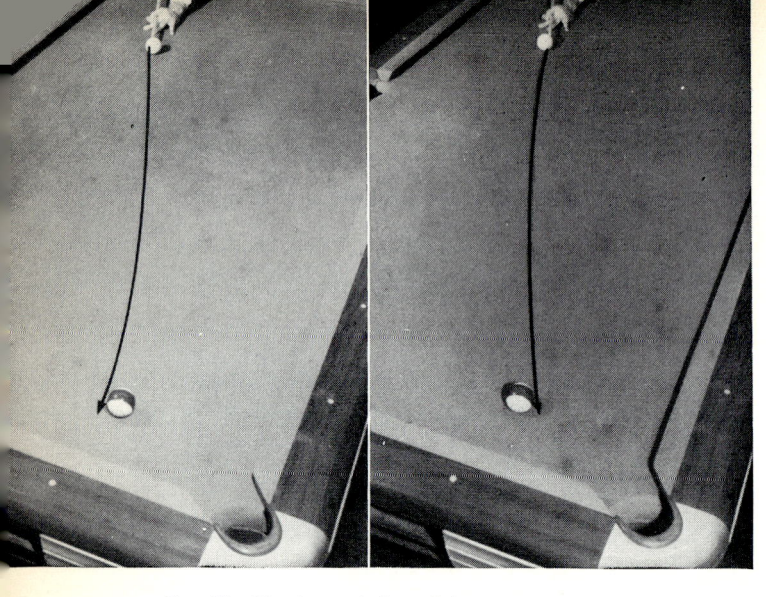

Figs. 31, 32. A cue ball Englished on the right curves to right at object ball. If struck on the left, it would curve to left.

may miss the ball entirely if he planned to make a thin hit on the left side of the object ball. To avoid the miss, he aims to hit more of the object ball, knowing the cue ball is curving away from his line of aim.

Draw and Follow

Now, we come to the most useful instruments at the command of a pocket billiard player — draw and follow. Unless the cueman can make the cue ball follow as he plans or draw as he plans, he'll never be a good position player. Unless he can play good position, he will never be a good pocket billiard player.

How often we have heard someone say about a player, "He's a great shotmaker, but he has to be. He's always shooting himself out of trouble." Such a player gets in trouble because he cannot control his cue ball for position play.

Control of the cue ball depends more on the ability to draw or follow than on any other factor, with the exception of speed of stroke.

Follow is accomplished by striking the cue ball above center; that is, above the horizontal axis of the ball (Fig. 33). Draw is achieved by striking the cue ball below center (Fig. 34). Again, draw and follow can be accomplished by striking the cue ball no more than a cue tip-width above or below center, assuming that the stroke is good.

On follow shots, I agree with the "no-more-than-cue-tip-width-above-center" rule. *But on draw shots, I advise striking the cue ball as low as reasonably possible. This is necessary to get the decisive draw action required in pocket billiards. Since, on a draw shot, most of the weight of the ball is above the point of aim, the lower you dig into the cue ball, the better you can bring the cue-ball weight back.*

Elevating Cue

Regardless of the positions of the cue ball and the object balls on the table, you will be able to shoot most of your follow shots with a reasonably level cue.

This is not always the case in draw shots, since the cue must be elevated when the player has to draw when the cue ball is near the rail or when he has to stroke over an object ball.

In Fig. 35, we see the cue ball very near the rail. The player elevates the butt end of his cue to draw the cue ball. In this case, the "horizontal" axis of the cue

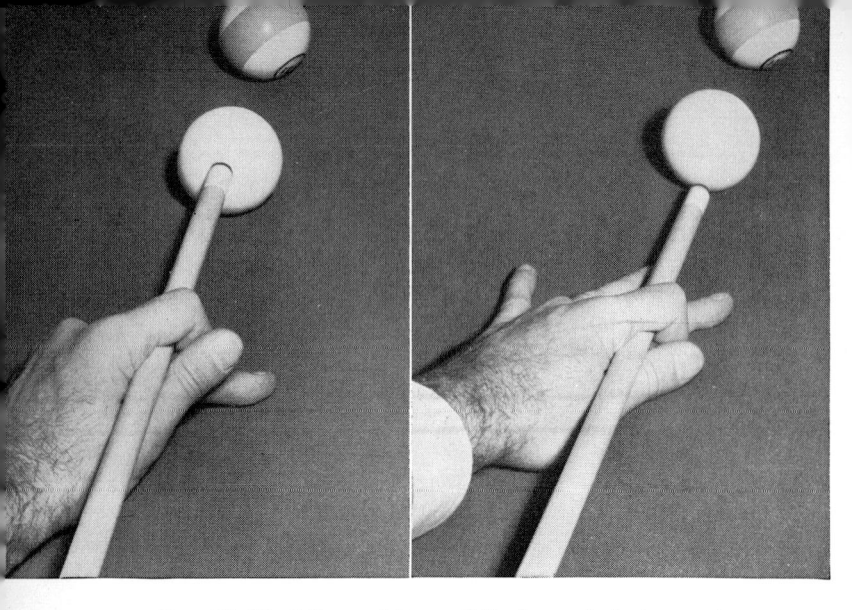

Figs. 33, 34. Follow and Draw. Strike the cue ball above center for Follow. Strike cue ball well below center point for Draw.

ball is parallel to the angle of cue elevation. Thus, if the player strikes down on the ball, hitting it below the axis, he will draw the ball. In Fig. 36, the player has a similar shot over an object ball. He is hitting below the axis of the cue ball and will draw it. *(Remember that solid bridge!)*

Stop-ball Stroke

It is essential, too, in pocket billiards that the player be able to execute a stop-ball shot, since many times during the course of a run, he will want to stop the cue ball "dead" at the point of contact with the object ball to leave himself in position to shoot one or more easy shots. The stop-ball effect is accomplished by stroking the cue ball in the exact center with a definite follow-through. The cue must be as level as you can possibly contrive to make it.

HORIZONTAL AXIS

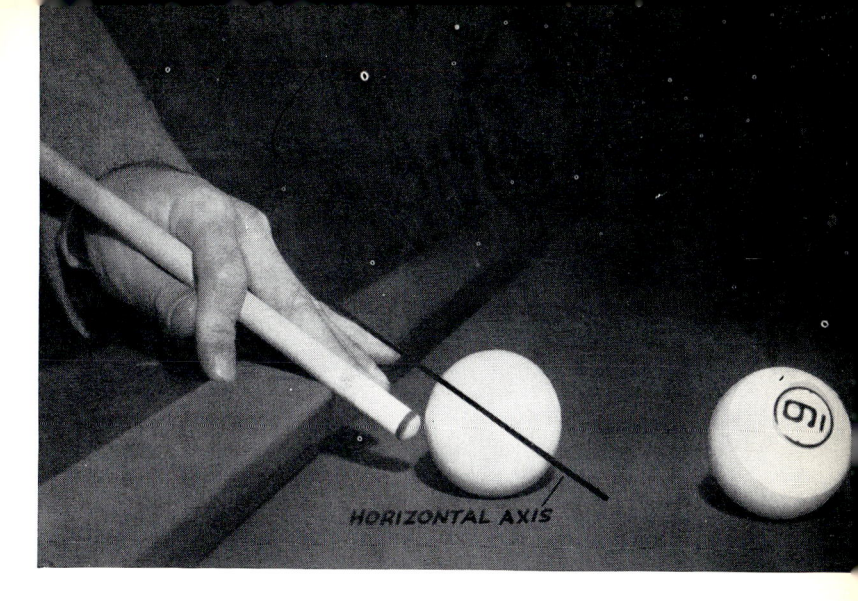

Fig. 35. Here the "horizontal" axis of the cue ball parallels cue elevation. You will draw ball by striking down on it below axis.

Fig. 36. A similar shot over an object ball. Hit below cue ball axis and draw shot. Note the solid bridge that is so important.

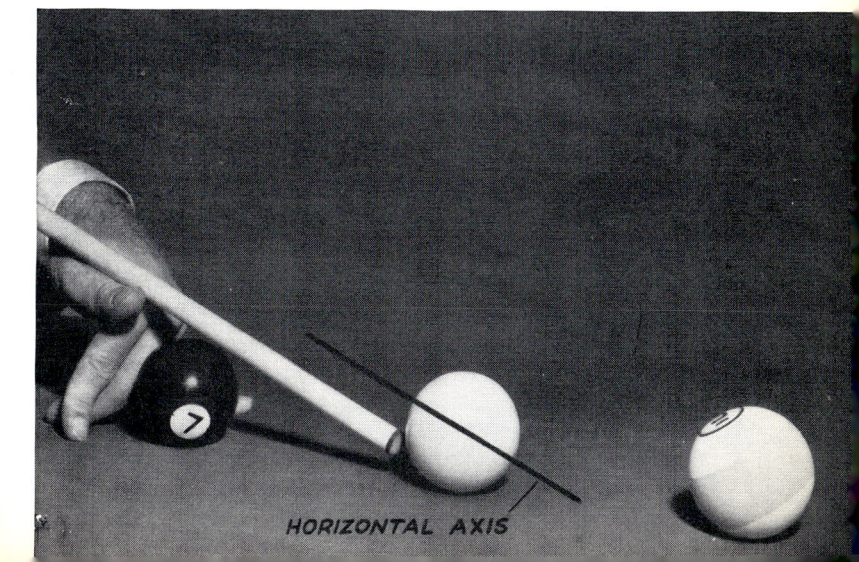

HORIZONTAL AXIS

LITTLE SPORTS LIBRARY

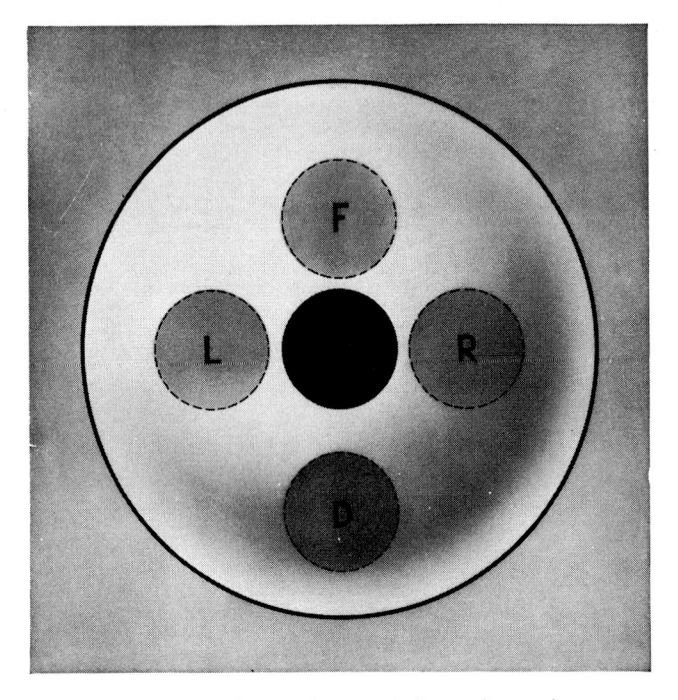

Fig. 37. Diagram indicates where cue ball must be struck to produce left (L) and right (R) English, follow (F), and draw (D).

Cue Ball and Stroke

Now that we have discussed center-ball, English, follow, draw, and stop-ball, the player has a pretty fair idea of how to cue the cue ball, but he must remember, too, that his stroke is important in cueing the ball. He must have a short, solid bridge, utilizing the best type of bridge for the shot in question.

He must decide where he will contact the cue ball

with the cue tip to get the best result on the shot. As he does his warm-up stroking, his attention shifts from the point on the cue ball he will contact to the point of aim on the object ball. Just before he strokes the cue ball, his eyes shift to the point of aim on the object ball, but the player knows, if his bridge is snug and firm, his stroke grooved, and the cue held as level as possible, he will strike the cue ball at the desired contact point, even though he is looking at the object ball.

Before we leave the subject of cueing the ball, we can study the drawing of Fig. 37 for guidance in where to strike the cue ball for English, right and left, and follow and draw. Remember, we strike the ball *as low as is reasonably possible on draw shots.*

6. Hitting the Object Ball

THE first thing the player must learn as he takes aim at object balls is that *his eyes are on the object ball when he strokes the cue ball*. We make this point because in the game of three-cushion billiards, for example, Champion Willie Hoppe looks at the cue ball last. In pocket billiards, however, we look at the *object ball* last, because we have less margin of error in our aim than is allowed in three-cushion billiards.

Sighting the Object Ball

Most players, even beginners, can sight an object ball with relation to the angle of aim and shoot the ball in the pocket. However, all shots can be figured mathematically, so to speak, so let's leave nothing to chance. Fig. 38 explains our point.

In this illustration we have set up an object-ball shot, which becomes progressively harder as we follow the pattern. Note that there are six cue balls on the table in shooting position. Also there is a cue ball in contact with the 15-ball, which is our object. The cue ball in contact with the object ball shows where the cue ball will contact that object ball in any of the six shots set up on the table.

Fig. 38. An object ball shot pattern. Cue ball in contact with object ball shows where balls will contact on any of six shots.

Fig. 39. This pattern starts from the left side. Contact point on cue ball stays same but more of object ball is hit each time.

LITTLE SPORTS LIBRARY

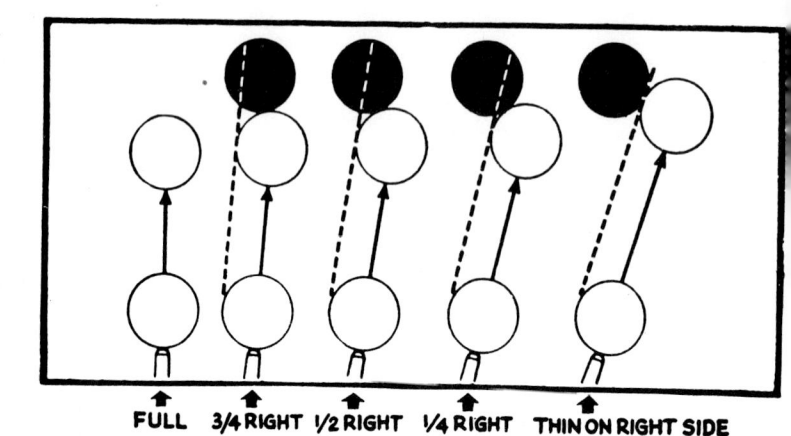

FULL 3/4 RIGHT 1/2 RIGHT 1/4 RIGHT THIN ON RIGHT SIDE

Fig. 40. Hits on the object ball, with diagram of a full-ball contact, three-quarter, one-half, one-quarter to thin on the right.

In the first shot (see cue behind ball), the player shoots a full-ball contact to drive the object ball straight ahead into the pocket. As he shoots the shots in order from his right to his left, he is cutting less of the object each time, until finally on the last shot he is "feathering" the object ball — that is, cutting it very thin.

In all these shots the contact point on the object ball is the same. The cue ball placed against the object ball proves this point. Fig. 39 is practically the same shot, starting from the player's left instead of his right. The point of contact on the cue ball is always the same, except that the player hits a little more object ball each time as he moves from left to right, aiming at that same point of contact.

52

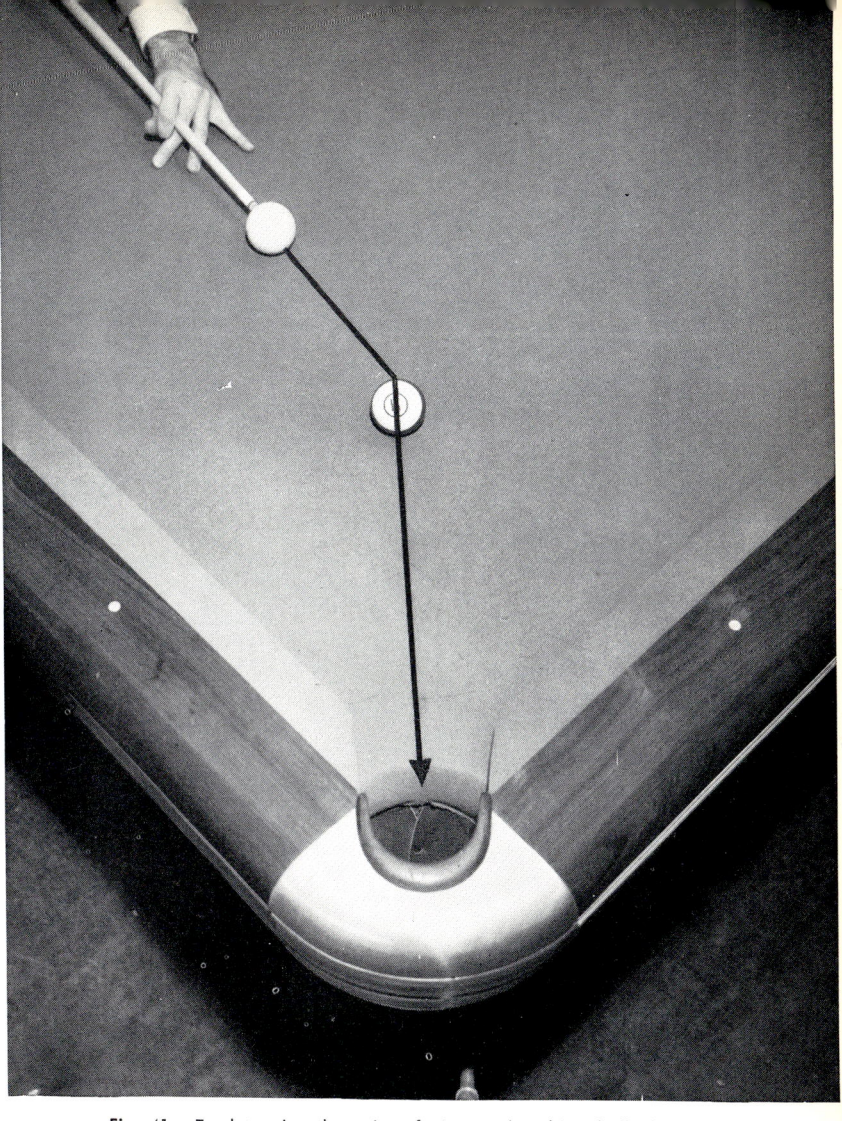

Fig. 41. To determine the point of aim on the object ball, draw a line from center of the pocket, which bisects the object ball.

Fig. 40 shows how the object ball must be cut, with reference to a full-ball contact, three-quarter hit, half-ball hit, etc.

Determining Point of Aim

The simplest way to determine the point of aim on the object ball is to draw a line from the center of the pocket which bisects the object ball (Fig. 41). Where this line extends through the object ball is the point of aim. If you can see this point of aim, as your head is in the line of aim over the cue, you can pocket the ball at any angle up to 180 degrees — that is, a straight line.

Hitting Point of Aim

Determining your point of aim is easy, but striking the ball at that point is another matter, especially when the shot requires a very thin hit. If the ball is close to the pocket, the permissible margin of error is considerable, but as the object ball is farther from the pocket, the permissible margin of error decreases, since the longer the roll of the ball, the more it may roll out of line (Fig. 42).

Here is where we come to the importance of striking the cue ball in the center. You will remember, in our discussion of English, we learned that the path of the cue ball is influenced by English. Thus, if you use English on the cue ball, your point of aim on the object ball varies according to the distance between cue ball and object ball. Also, you learned under "English" that English on the cue ball influences the roll of the object ball.

The lines in Fig. 42 indicate how the ball would travel to the pocket on a faulty aim — a too-full hit on the object ball, in this case. Even though the aim

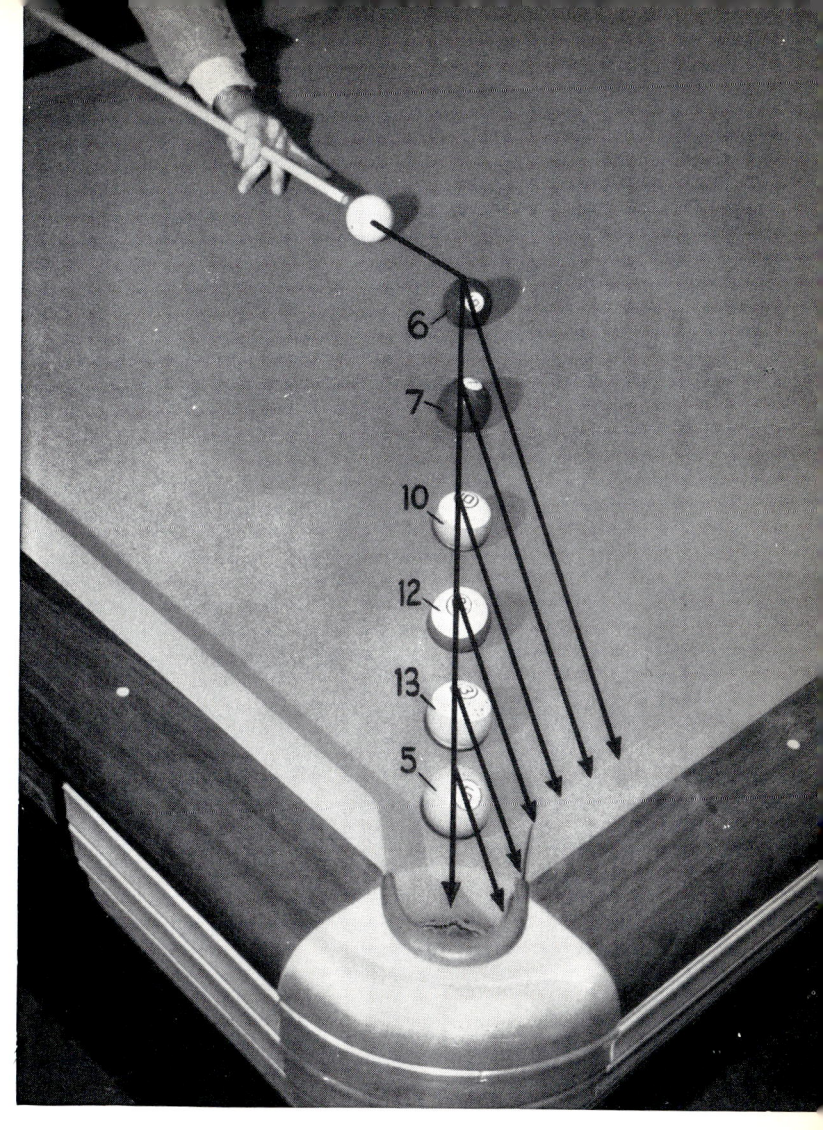

Fig. 42. Margin of error increases the farther the object ball is from the pocket. Lines show paths of ball with faulty aim.

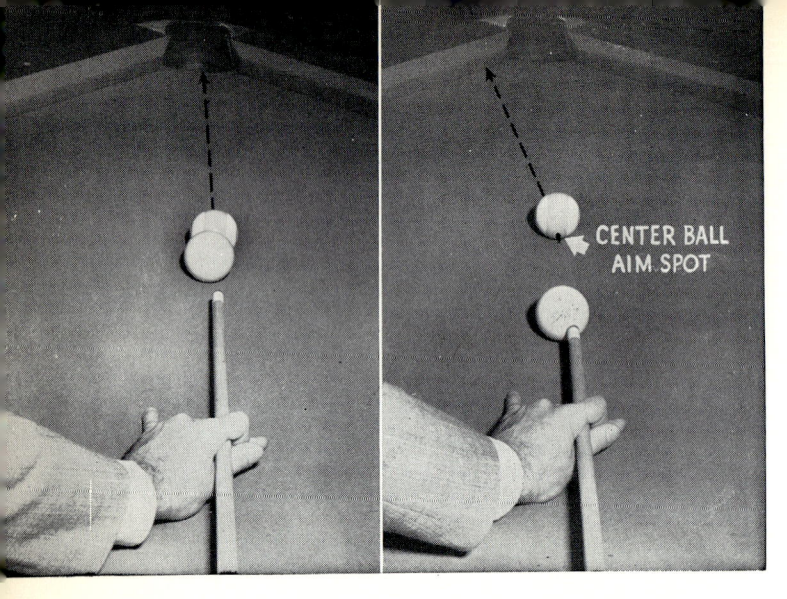

Figs. 43, 44. English influences the object ball. If you hit cue ball on left, object ball is thrown to right. Hitting cue ball on right gives opposite effect. See text for proper use of English.

were faulty, as in this case, the 5-ball would score, as would the 13-ball. But the 12-ball might miss. The 10-, 7- and 6-balls definitely would miss. The point of aim on all object balls is the same, since a line drawn from the center of the pocket bisects all the object balls at the same relative spot. This picture illustrates how the permissible margin of error decreases, the farther the object ball is from the pocket.

Influence of English on Object Ball

Here is how English affects the object ball. If you cue the cue ball on the left, the object ball is thrown to the right. If you cue the cue ball with right English, the object ball is thrown to the left (Figs. 43, 44).

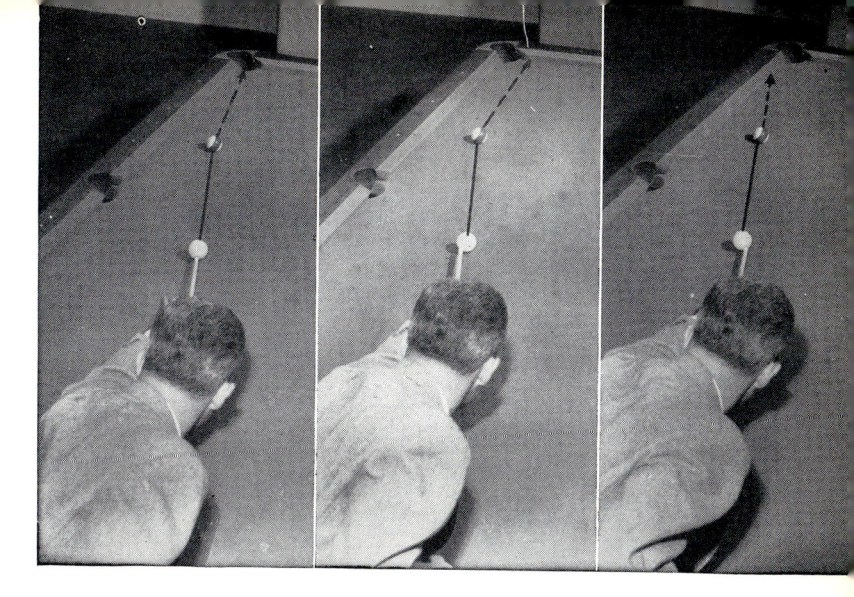

Figs. 45, 46, 47. When using English, allow for it on your point of aim. Pictures show center shot, English left and right shots. Throw of English on object ball increases with length of shot.

Thus, never use English on a shot unless:

1. You want to throw the object ball.
2. When playing for position, you want to make the cue ball take English off a rail — either natural or reverse English.

Again, we emphasize the value of center-ball stroking, but, admitting English is required in some situations, we must understand its influence on the object ball.

If you want to use English you must allow for it on your point of aim. Figs. 45, 46, and 47 illustrate our point. If in Fig. 45 we hit the object ball at the proper point of aim with no English, the ball will travel into the pocket as indicated. If we hit the ball at the same

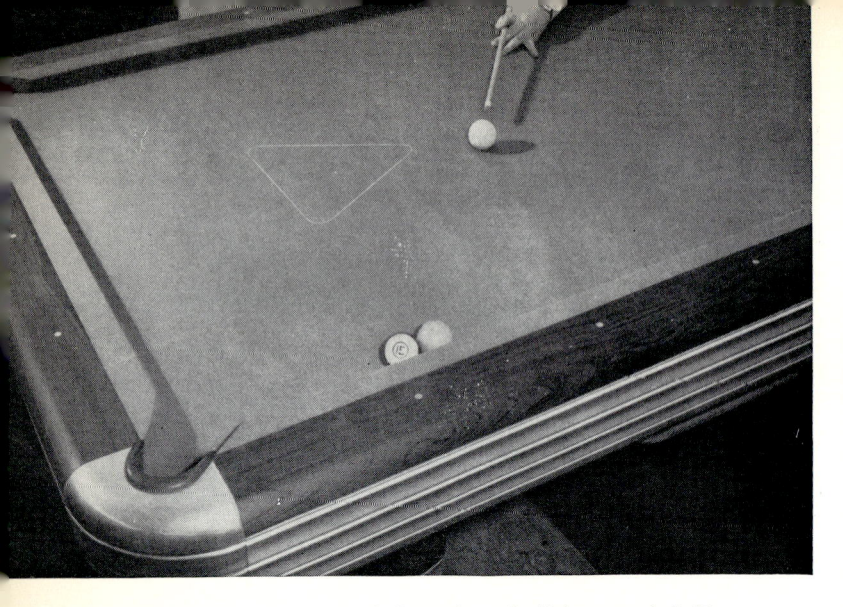

Fig. 48. Shooting object ball on the rail. Make center-ball hit on cue ball, aiming for object ball and cushion at the same time.

Fig. 49. Here a very thin hit on the object ball is required for success. Hit cushion first, with right English on the cue ball.

point of aim with English left, the object ball will be thrown to the right, as indicated in Fig. 46. English on the right of the cue ball, will throw the object ball to the left, as shown in Fig. 47.

Always remember that the throw of English on the object balls increases in proportion to the length of the shot. The throw will be slight in a short shot; it can be as much as four inches off the apparent line of aim on a long shot.

Hitting Object Ball on Rail

The proper way to shoot at an object ball on the rail is illustrated in Figs. 48 and 49. The shot demonstrated in Fig. 48 is comparatively simple. It can be made with center-ball stroke on the cue ball, the player aiming to hit the object ball and the cushion at the same time. It is evident that the player cannot hit the object ball too full. If he does, the ball will tend to bounce out from the cushion.

The shot set up in Fig. 49 is more difficult, since it requires a very thin hit on the object ball. Most top-flight players, shooting this shot, would hit the cushion first, within an eyelash of the object ball, cueing the cue ball with left English. English left, we know, throws the object ball to the right. Thus, in cueing this shot with left English, the object ball is thrown to the right — that is, it will hug the rail as it travels to the pocket.

7. Combination and Kiss Shots

Combination Shots

NO matter how skillful a player becomes in the game of pocket billiards, he will frequently get into trouble during a run. Often a combination shot is his only hope of continuing his run. Thus, the player should understand combinations and be able to recognize quickly if the combination "is on." If it isn't "on," he should abandon the shot and resort to safety, since if he shoots the shot and misses, he spreads the balls and, more often than not, leaves a shot for his opponent.

Fig. 50 sets up a combination that is "on" the pocket, even though the 1-ball (the called ball) appears to be headed for the 15-ball instead of the pocket (see broken line 1). This shot is made by hitting the first ball on the combination to the right of center. As the first ball in the combination hits the 1-ball, it will throw the 1-ball to the left into the pocket. The balls in this combination are frozen, but the shot can be made when the balls are as far as (but no farther than) a quarter of an inch apart. If the balls are separated, the first ball in the combination is hit slightly closer to center.

The player should understand the "throw" of the

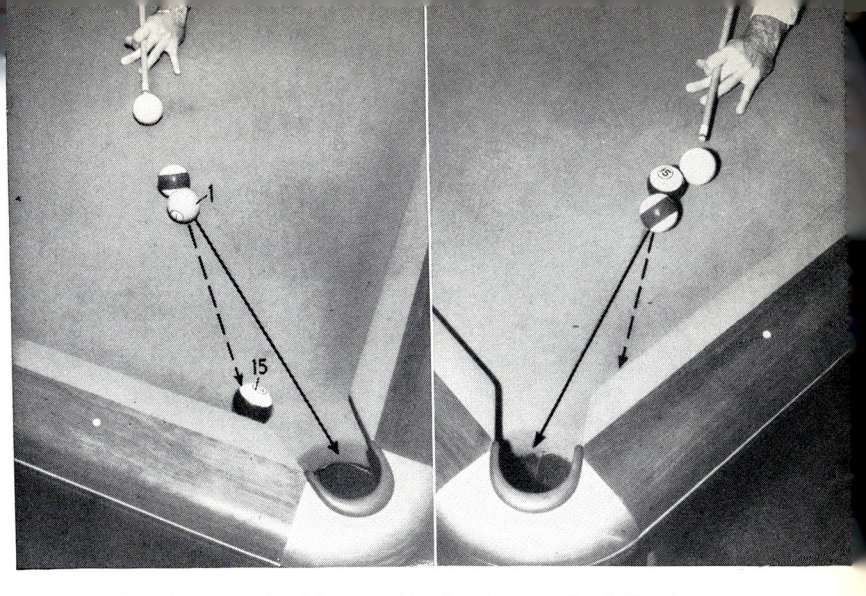

Figs. 50, 51. Both of these combination shots are "on." See the accompanying text for details on how each should be carried out.

balls on this combination. If the key ball hits the second object ball on the left, the called ball is thrown to the right; if it hits it on the right, the called object ball is thrown to the left.

The combination in Fig. 51 is "on," also. By hitting the first ball in the combination on the left side, we throw the called ball, which seems headed into the rail to the left of the pocket (broken line), to the right and into the pocket (solid line).

A three-ball combination, which is on, is illustrated in Fig. 52. This combination is possible because the key ball, the third (or dark ball) in the combination, is properly placed. If this were a two-ball combination, we would try to hit the second ball with the cue ball just as the dark ball will be driven into the second

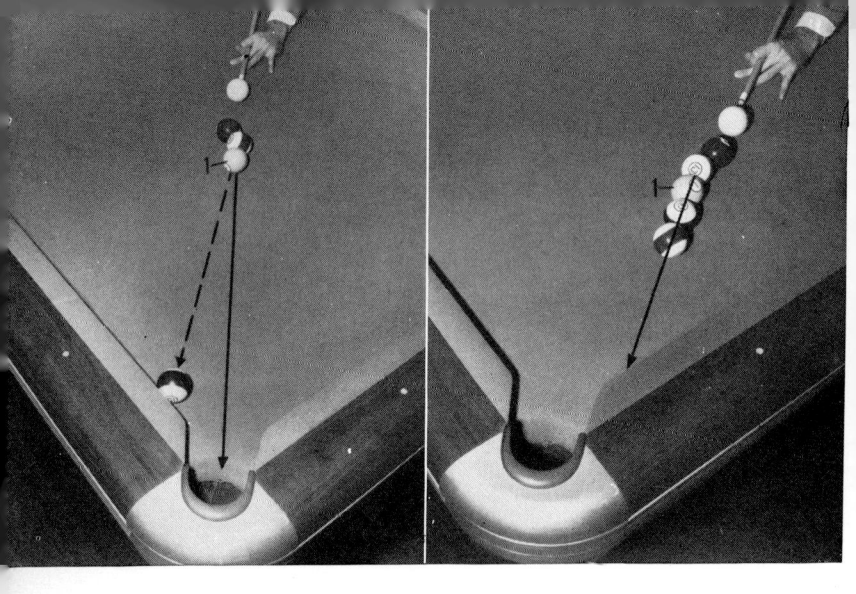

Figs. 52, 53. The three-ball combination (left) is "on" while the five-ball combination (right) is not. See text for details.

ball on this shot. After contact is made on this line of aim, the 1-ball (the called ball), will be thrown to the left into the pocket.

Remember, when three or more object balls are involved in a combination, *the third ball is always the key ball.* To ascertain which is the "third" ball, start with the called ball as "one," the next one to it in the combination as "two," and the next one to that as "three." The latter is your key ball. Fig. 53 illustrates a five-ball combination.

This shot is not "on" because the position of the third or "key" ball (1-ball) is such that it will drive the called ball into the left rail.

In Fig. 54, the five-ball combination is "on," because the third ball (the key ball) is in proper position. The 1-ball, hitting the 15-ball on the left

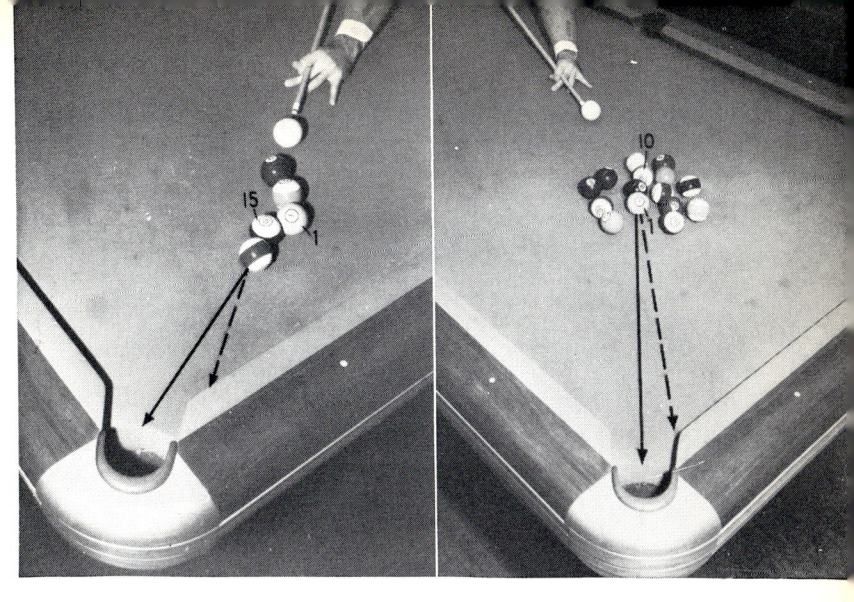

Figs. 54, 55. Both of these combinations are "on." Picture at right shows possible setup after opening break shot has been made.

side, will throw the called ball to the right.

Fig. 55 shows a situation which might arise after the player has made the opening break shot. At first glance the player seems to be without a shot, but study of the clustered balls reveals a combination. The third (10-) ball in the combination is in proper position to pocket the called (1-) ball. The called ball is "on" the pocket at the bottom of the picture.

A player, however, will never learn all about combination shots from a pocket billiard book. He must set up shots on the table for himself, practicing until he learns the possibilities. The important thing to remember is that if the combination involves three or more object balls, the third ball is always the key ball.

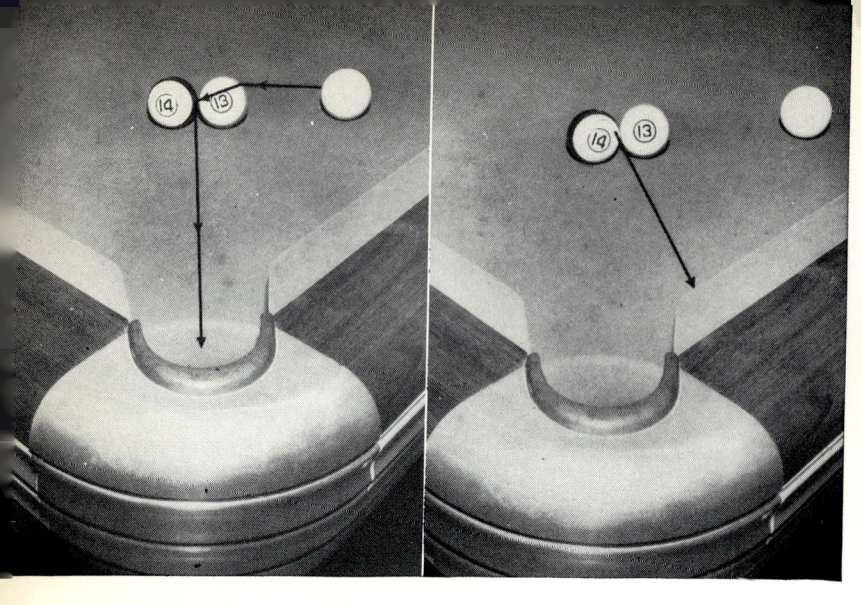

Figs. 56, 57. Line drawn from between two balls indicates that kiss shot at left is "on;" one at right is not, but can be made.

Kiss Shots

A kiss shot is just the opposite, in a manner of speaking, from a combination shot. In a combination, you drive an object ball into the called ball. In a kiss shot, you make the called ball carom off an object ball.

Fig. 56 shows a kiss shot which is on. The player may make this shot by driving his cue ball into the 13-ball (the called ball), driving the 13-ball into the 14-ball, from which it will kiss into the pocket in the foreground.

This shot is "on" because a line drawn from the middle of the pocket runs between the two balls, as illustrated. In Fig. 57, the shot is not "on," because a line running between the two balls runs into the

64

left rail, as diagrammed. This kiss shot can be made, however, by striking the cue ball with a draw stroke, which would force the 13-ball (called ball) slightly forward as it caroms off the 14-ball.

Again, the player must set up kiss shots and practice them until he learns which shots are on and which aren't. If the player applies the "line measurement," as we have in Figs. 56 and 57, he will have a fairly accurate gauge of the possibilities of pocketing a kiss shot, regardless of where the balls are placed.

Remember, if the kiss shot is on according to your gauge, play it with center-ball on the vertical axis of the cue ball. If you want to force the called ball forward, use a draw stroke. If you want to carom the called ball back off an object ball, use a follow stroke.

Other kiss shots, with the object balls separated, are set up in Figs. 58, 59, and 60. In Fig. 58, the 13-ball can be pocketed by caroming it off the 14-ball. The shot requires about a four-fifths full hit on the pocket side of the 14-ball.

The shot in Fig. 59 requires a thinner carom; that is, the cue ball would drive the 13-ball into the 14-ball on a one-half-ball contact, driving the 13-ball into the right corner pocket.

A three-ball kiss shot is illustrated in Fig. 60. The 15-ball is the called ball. First, it will strike 13-ball, caroming into 14-ball, and thence into pocket in foreground.

Bank Shots

Bank shots are never regarded as easy, and a player seldom tries them in a championship game, except as a last resort. Unless the player is quite certain he can make the bank shot, he should abandon it and play

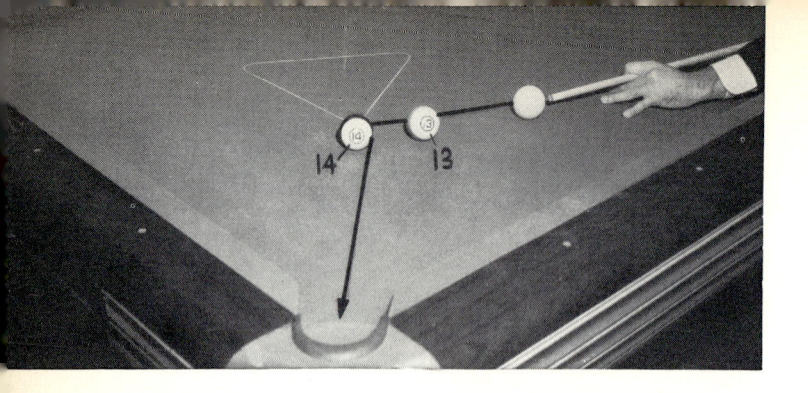

Fig. 58. Above: Pocket 13-ball by caroming it off the 14-ball.

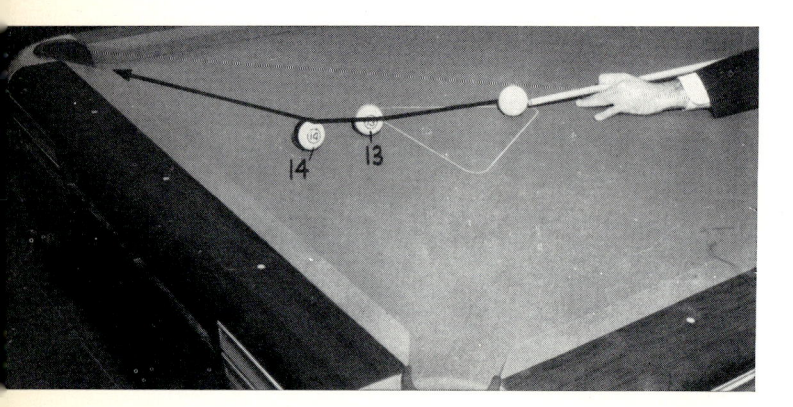

Fig. 59. Above: Here a thinner carom is needed to pocket 13-ball.

Fig. 60. Three-ball kiss shot where 15-ball caroms off 13 and 14.

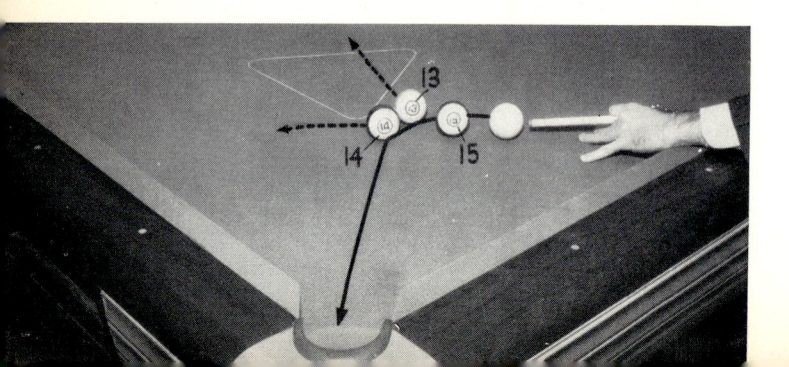

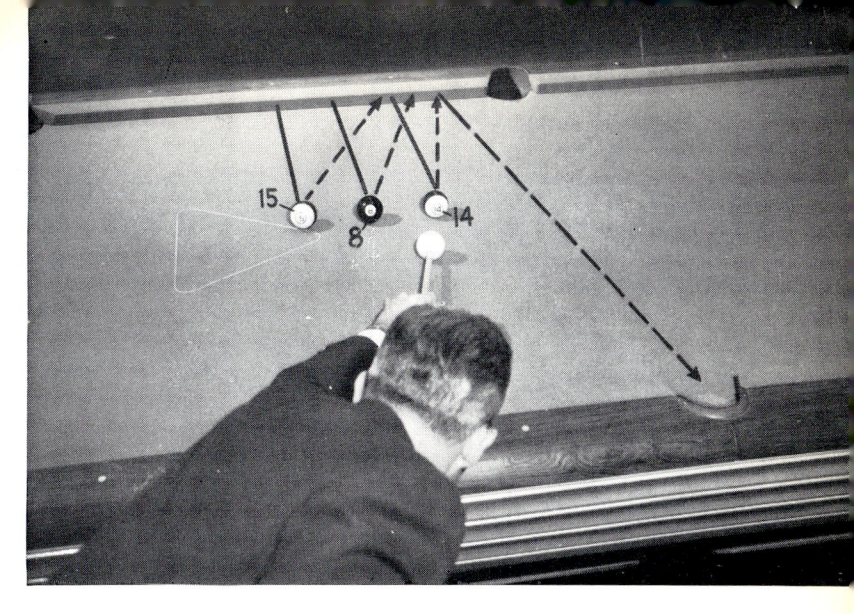

Fig. 61. How to play bank shots. See text for details. The dotted lines here show how to pocket each of the three balls.

safe, unless the position of the balls on the table denies him a better "percentage" than the bank shot offers.

Bank shots can be figured rather accurately, by "bisecting the angle," as shown in Fig. 61. Note that the 14-ball is on a line which runs across the table through the first diamonds on this side of the side pockets. "Bisecting the angle," the player arrives at a point halfway between the diamond and the side pocket.

He would strike the halfway point between the diamond and the side pocket to bank the shot across the table, as diagrammed.

The 8-ball is a diamond and one-half from the side pocket. Bisecting the angle — or dividing 1½ by 2 — the player gets ¾ of a diamond from the side pocket, where he would drive the 8-ball to bank it in the right side pocket.

The 15-ball is on a line running between the second diamonds from the side pockets. Bisecting the angle, the player would drive the 15-ball into the one diamond on the far rail to bank it into the near side pocket.

Bank shots are shot with a medium hard stroke, since the player wants the banked ball to travel the exact path he planned for it. As the angle of the bank widens, the stroke is harder, since the ball approaching the rail at a wide angle may drift off that rail at a wider angle if the stroke is too soft. Use center-ball stroke.

8. The Championship Game

SO far we have covered the various **fundamentals** of the game. Also, we have examined the subjects of center-ball stroking, follow, draw, stop ball, English, hitting the object ball, influence of English on object ball, combinations, and kiss shots.

If the player is well schooled in the phases of the game covered and can execute his shots with reasonable skill, he is ready to play the **championship poc**ket billiard game of 14.1 rack.

This is the championship game because it calls for all the resources of the pocket billiard player's skill. As the player runs even one frame of balls from the table, he may be confronted with situations which require skillful stroking and a complete knowledge of the game.

We now have reached the point in this discussion where the player must go to the table and play the championship game. We don't expect that beginning players will run off a frame of balls during their first inning at the table, nor do we expect that average players will blossom into stardom overnight.

We have, however, told you what to do and how to do. Now it is up to you. You must put these lessons into practice at the table. And the best way to practice is to play the game. Later, we will go into the more advanced phases of position play, but for the present, let us play 14.1 rack.

Fig. 62. Opening break shot. The 1- and 10-balls are driven to cushions. Rule is that two object balls must hit cushions.

Fig. 63. At first glance, break used in Fig. 62 has left no shot. But 1-ball can be pocketed as shown with 3-ball as key (see text).

Opening Break Shot

In 14.1-rack pocket billiards the 15 object balls are racked in a pyramid at the foot spot and the player has the cue ball in hand behind the head string (Fig. 62).

The requirements of the opening break shot are that the player drive at least two object balls to the cushions. (See 14.1-rack rules, page 130.)

It is possible to call a ball on the opening break shot and pocket the ball as called, but the chances of making a called ball are so remote that the player resorts to safety. (See "Safety Requirements," page 136.)

I play the opening break shot as follows: The cue ball is placed on the head string halfway between the head spot and the right side rail (the rail to my right — Fig. 62). I stroke the cue ball with right English slightly above center. It is my intention to hit the corner ball (the 1-ball) in the pyramid very thin, but since I know the ball Englished on the right side will curve to the right, I play to hit the 1-ball one-third full, allowing for the curve.

My intention on the shot is to drive the 1-ball to the foot cushion and the 10-ball to the left side (Fig. 62). If I play the shot well I will accomplish this intention, disturbing the rack but slightly and bringing the 1- and 10-balls back close to the rack. This denies my opponent a shot.

The cue ball, meanwhile, hits at about the three-fourths diamond on the foot rail, travels to the one diamond on the right rail, bounds to the seven diamond on the left rail and comes to a stop about three-quarters of a diamond from the left rail on the head cushion.

How well I have accomplished my purpose is shown in Fig. 63. To all appearances my opponent has no shot.

Thus, left "safe," the first thing the incoming player does is study the rack for a possible combination. And there is one! The 1-ball is "on" the corner pocket. This is apparent in Fig. 63, since the 3-ball — key ball in the combination — lies in proper position.

Pocketing the 1-ball on the combination, the player will spread the rack and should be in position to set off on a run.

Safety after Opening Break

More often than not, however, the player will be left without a reasonable shot, if his opponent breaks the balls properly and brings the cue ball down to the head cushion as shown in Fig. 63. When this happens, the incoming player has no sensible alternative but to play a return safety.

He may play a return safety in one of a dozen or more ways. Several possibilities are diagrammed in Figs. 64, 65, and 66 seen on Page 73.

The requirements of safety play in this instance (see rules) are that a player drive an object ball to a cushion or cause his cue ball to contact a cushion after hitting an object ball (or pocket an object ball).

Often, as a result of the cue ball coming to stop against the rack (Fig. 67) or as the result of a safety or scratch on the part of an opponent, the player will have no alternative but to play a safety off the clustered balls. His strategy, here, is to play a legal safety by skimming a ball in the rack and driving the cue ball as close to the head rail (far rail) as pos-

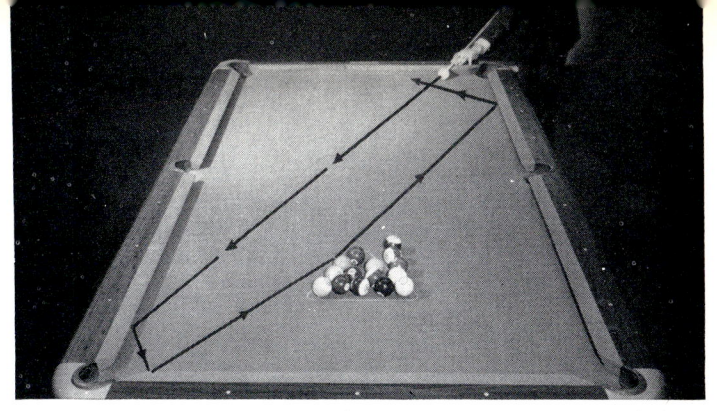

Fig. 64. Here is one way of playing a return safety if required.

Figs. 65, 66. More safety plays. Drive object ball to cushion or cause cue ball to hit cushion after hitting an object ball.

LITTLE SPORTS LIBRARY

sible. If he achieves this, the cue ball will come to rest as shown in Figs. 68 and 69. The rack has not been disturbed to any appreciable degree and the incoming player is confronted with a difficult situation.

The contesting players will play safe or scratch (see rules) until an object ball is left out and the cue ball comes to rest in a position which assures the incoming player a reasonable shot (Fig. 70). If he calls and pockets the shot, the game is under way.

Shooting Away

As the players resort to safety as discussed above, shots which are tempting will present themselves. The shrewd player, however, lets his opponent shoot the "impossible" ones. Don't elect to shoot a hard, long shot in this situation unless you are reasonably sure you can pocket the called ball. A miss may be fatal in these pocket billiard days of high runs. On the other hand, if a shot presents itself that you feel that you can make, shoot away. The point is: don't be foolhardy — but don't be fainthearted, either.

Be cautious about shooting away when it is difficult to cue the cue ball. Long shots — when the cue ball is resting against the head cushion or near the head cushion — are difficult if it is hard to cue the cue ball.

If you think you are right, have the courage and confidence of your conviction. We stress "courage" and "confidence" because you must have complete faith that you can make the shot. You can't tighten up and "dog it."

Also, be careful after you elect to shoot away that

Fig. 67. When cue ball stops against rack you must play a safety off the cluster. See next page for explanation of how it is done.

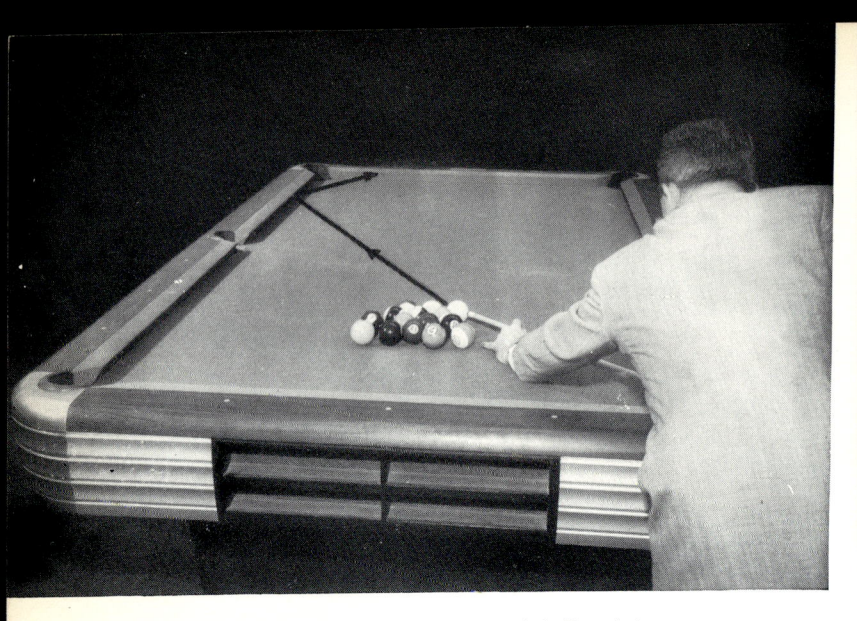

Fig. 68. A safety play. Cue ball skims rack ball and hits as close to head rail as possible. This is a good return safety.

Fig. 69. Cue ball rests along head rail. The rack has not been disturbed and your opponent is confronted with a difficult shot.

Fig. 70. Play safe or scratch until an object ball is left out and cue ball is in position for reasonable shot, to open game.

there is no danger of scratching the cue ball in a pocket. If there is, abandon the shot. Play safe. And if you decide to shoot away on a hard shot, determine before you do what the possibilities are for position for subsequent shots. If position is remote, abandon the shot. Play safe. Let your opponent shoot the tough ones.

Position Play

When the player gets the cue ball down within the foot-half of the table (near the rack) and has one or several open shots, he is ready to play position. If some of the balls are still clustered, he must maneuver around until he can use one of his open shots for a break ball. Fig. 71 shows a situation where-

77

Fig. 71. In this situation, you can pocket the 13-ball, get in position for the 14-ball, and break the cluster off the 8-ball.

in the player knows he can pocket the 13-ball, get in position for the 14-ball, and break the cluster off the 8-ball.

Position Play Strategy

As soon as the rack is spread, with no balls clustered, the player determines what object ball he will leave for his break shot. He then selects a key ball, which he will pocket last, knowing that after he pockets the key ball he will be in a relatively good position to shoot the break ball (Fig. 72).

In this situation the player would make the 13-ball his break ball. The 12-ball is the key ball. He would proceed as follows: Pocket the 11-ball in the corner, stop; play 15-ball in corner, follow to cushion and out

78

Fig. 72. When rack is spread, position-play strategy becomes essential. Text describes how to pocket string, with 13-ball last.

Fig. 73. Stop-ball technique will permit clearing table here. Start with 15-ball, then pocket, 2, 8, 11, and 6 in that order.

slightly; play 10-ball opposite corner, draw slightly for position on 9-ball; pocket 9-ball in side pocket, stop; 14-ball in corner, stop; 12-ball in side, stop; use 13-ball for break ball, with cue ball in good position.

Value of Stop Ball

The best way to play a frame of balls is the easiest way. Many times, with five or six balls remaining on the table, the player can pocket five of them and be in good position on his break ball *without going to a cushion*. During the run of five he may use follow or draw, but on many occasions he can get by with a stop-ball stroke, stopping the cue ball "dead" upon contact with the object ball. (Remember: a stop-ball stroke is executed by *striking the cue ball in dead center with a follow-through*.)

In Fig. 73, the player can clear the table with stop-ball play by: pocketing the 15-ball and stopping the cue ball dead; pocketing the 2-, then the 8-, and finally the 11-ball, leaving the cue ball in position to break off the 6-ball.

9. How Much Do You Know?

BY this time, the player should have a good idea of position play and should know how to size up the spread balls to proceed on his run. So, let's make the next few pages a "quiz program." See Fig. 74. How would you proceed on your run? Which is your break ball? Which is the key ball? We'll give you the correct answer below, but figure out the strategy of play yourself before reading the answer.

Answer: This problem can also be solved with stop-ball stroking. The player pockets the 8-ball in the corner; the 2-ball in the side; the 14-ball in the corner; the 11-ball in the side; and the 6-ball in the corner. Thus, he has good position on the 15-ball, for a side pocket break. The 6-ball was the key ball.

Another position-play problem is presented in Fig. 75. How would you proceed? Which is the break ball? Which is the key ball?

Answer: Shoot 11-ball in side, stop; 15-ball in corner, stop; 6-ball in side, with left-follow for position on 8-ball; 8-ball in corner, stop; 2-ball in corner, follow to side rail and out for position on 14-ball, which is break ball.

How would you clear the table in Fig. 76? Study the picture and solve this position-play problem before reading the answer.

Answer: Shoot 6-ball in corner, follow to cushion

Figs. 74, 75. Here are two position-play problems. QUESTION: Which are the "key" balls and "break" balls? Work out your own plan of attack before referring to the instructions in this chapter.

for straight on 14-ball; 14-ball in corner, stop for angle on 2-ball; cut 2-ball in corner, with follow, going into side cushion and coming off for position on 7-ball; cut 7-ball same corner, coming out slightly from rail; shoot 4-ball in side (across table), stop; 11-ball in side, stop; 15-ball in side, stop for position on 8-ball, which is break ball.

In Fig. 77, a more difficult problem is posed. As the balls lie, there isn't a good break ball on the table. How would you proceed in this situation?

Answer: In this shot, I would manufacture my break shot, proceeding as follows: Shoot the 2-ball in the corner, stop; the 7-ball in the side, stop; the 4-ball in the corner, stop. At this point, the three balls remaining on the table are placed as in Fig. 78. Now, you cut the 6-ball in corner, caroming off it to strike the 8-ball, driving the 8-ball a few inches nearer to the right rail (right rail as you study the picture).

If you accomplish your purpose, the balls will come to rest as shown in Fig. 79. You shoot the 11-ball in side, stop, getting good position for a break shot off the 8-ball.

Our final problem for position play is set up in Fig. 80. What would you do? Where is your break ball? What about the two balls clustered on the right rail?

Answer: Play the 2-ball in the corner, stop (Fig. 81). Play 6-ball in corner, cutting cue ball into cushion behind the 8-ball. If you are successful the balls will come to rest as shown in Fig. 82. The 8-ball has come to rest in position for a good break shot. Now pocket 4-ball in corner, using soft two-cushion follow. Pocket 14-ball in side, using stop stroke. You proceed, pocketing 11-ball in the corner (Fig. 83), drawing cue ball to cushion and coming off for your

Fig. 76. QUESTION: How would you clear this table? Study the picture awhile and then solve this good-position-play problem.

Fig. 77. A more difficult case with no apparent break ball. QUESTION: How would you "manufacture" your own break shot?

Fig. 78. After you pocket three balls (Fig. 77), there are three balls still remaining on the table. P r o c e e d from there.

Fig. 79. Balls should rest in this position after following up on Fig. 78. Your next play sets up good position for break shot.

Fig. 80. QUESTION: Where is your break ball? How will you handle the two balls on the right rail? Outline your play.

break shot (Fig. 84). Referring back to Fig. 80, the 4-ball was the key ball in this situation. Why?

It was necessary to keep the 4-ball on the table, until after your attempt to drive the 8-ball away from the rail. Had you failed to move the 8-ball out for a break shot, the 4-ball would have been your alternative break shot.

Practice Shots

In Figs. 85, 86, 87, and 88, we have set up practice shots, which will help the player bring his cue ball off the key ball into position for the break ball.

We will pause here to emphasize that good position on the break ball is the most important single factor in high runs in pocket billiards. Any good shotmaker can run 14 balls off the table, but the fellow who con-

Figs. 81, 82. Beginning of solution to problem shown in Fig. 80. This is real position play. Shot indicated above should leave setup illustrated below. Remaining steps are shown on next page.

Figs. 83, 84. Windup of series begun in Fig. 80. Pocket 11-ball in corner (Fig. 81), coming off cushion into good position for break shot on 8-ball (Fig. 82). See text on page 83 for details.

tinues his run from rack to rack is the fellow who gets good position on the break ball. Practice the shots diagrammed in Figs. 85, 86, 87, and 88.

In Fig. 85, the player strokes the cue ball with follow, English slightly left. He should practice this shot as diagrammed until he can bring the cue ball to rest on a square of paper or reasonably close to it.

In Fig. 86, the player cues the ball with follow, using no English. The cue ball crosses the table as diagrammed (three-cushion contacts) to come to rest on or close to the piece of paper.

In Fig. 87, the player cues the ball with follow, using no English. The cue ball travels to the paper as diagrammed.

In Fig. 88, player cues the ball with follow, using no English. Cue ball travels as diagrammed.

If the player practices shots such as these until he has mastered them, he will have solved the most important secret of high runs.

How To Play Break Shots

On the following pages, we have set up a number of break shots, explaining how they are made.

Fig. 89 demonstrates the best of all break shots. The player has a relatively simple object-ball shot and he can carom off the break ball into the pyramid with little difficulty. He strokes the cue ball with follow, using no English. The carom should take the cue ball into rack between the 2- and 12-balls. Follow action on the cue ball will cause the cue ball to fight its way into the rack, spreading the object balls.

The player is straighter on the break ball in Fig. 90. He still has a good break shot, however. He strokes the cue ball slightly above center, with right English. The

Fig. 85. Stroke cue ball with follow, English slightly left. Practice until you bring cue ball to rest on a square of paper.

Fig. 86. Cue the ball with follow, no English. Cue ball goes across table to come to rest on or close to the piece of paper.

Fig. 87. Cue the ball with follow, using no English. Cue ball should travel to the piece of paper as the black line indicates.

Fig. 88. Ball travels course as in Fig. 87, though in another direction. Work on these practice shots until you master them.

English carries the cue ball between the 2- and 12-balls with added momentum. The cue ball then travels to the foot rail and off, as diagrammed.

A side-pocket break is illustrated in Fig. 91. Use English left, cueing ball in center of vertical axis. Cue ball travels as diagrammed.

Fig. 92 shows the break ball behind the rack. Use follow; no English. Cue ball travels as diagrammed.

The cue ball is straighter with the break ball in Fig. 93. Player cues the ball slightly above center with left English. Note course of cue ball.

Another side-pocket break shot is demonstrated in Fig. 94. Cue ball in dead center (center of vertical and horizontal axes). *Hold the cue level.* Cue ball caroms off break ball into pyramid as diagrammed.

To make break shot illustrated in Fig. 95, player cues ball with low, right English. Cue ball rolls as indicated.

Care must be exercised in break shot illustrated in Fig. 96 to strike the object ball at the point of aim. Cue ball in dead center. Hold cue level. Cue ball strikes pyramid as indicated.

Break shot in Fig. 97 is shot with draw, English left. Cue ball takes diagrammed path.

In Fig. 98, shot is made with follow, English left. Cue ball takes diagrammed path, fighting its way into rack, spreading the balls.

The diagrams shown in Figs. 89 through 98, inclusive, indicate how the top-flight player tries to play the break shots. No player is assured that he will get the desired action every time he shoots the shot, but if the player practices until he can shoot the shots as diagrammed with a fair degree of success, he will be on the right road to high runs in pocket billiards.

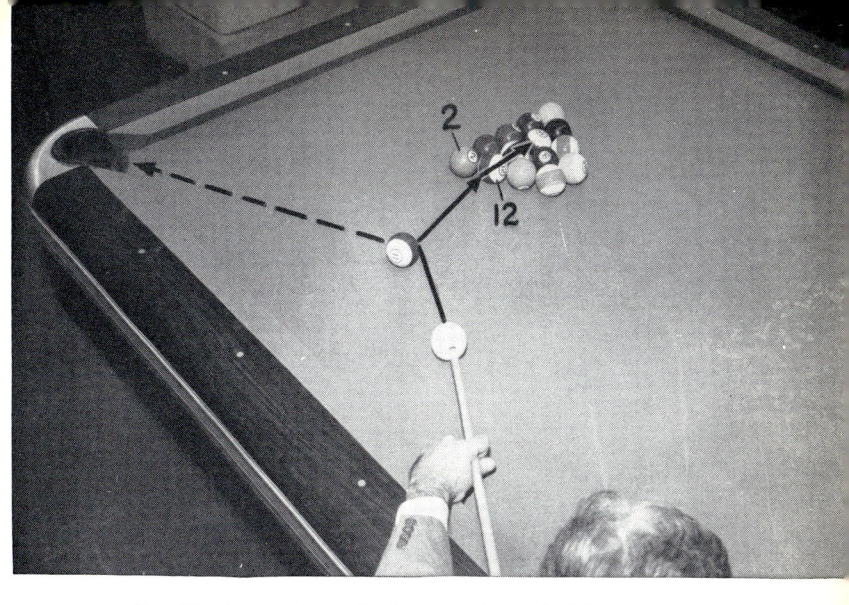

Fig. 89. Here is best of all break shots. A follow stroke on cue ball causes it to follow into rack, spreading object balls.

Fig. 90 Another break shot stroked slightly above center, with right English; cue ball hits rack, travels to foot rail and off.

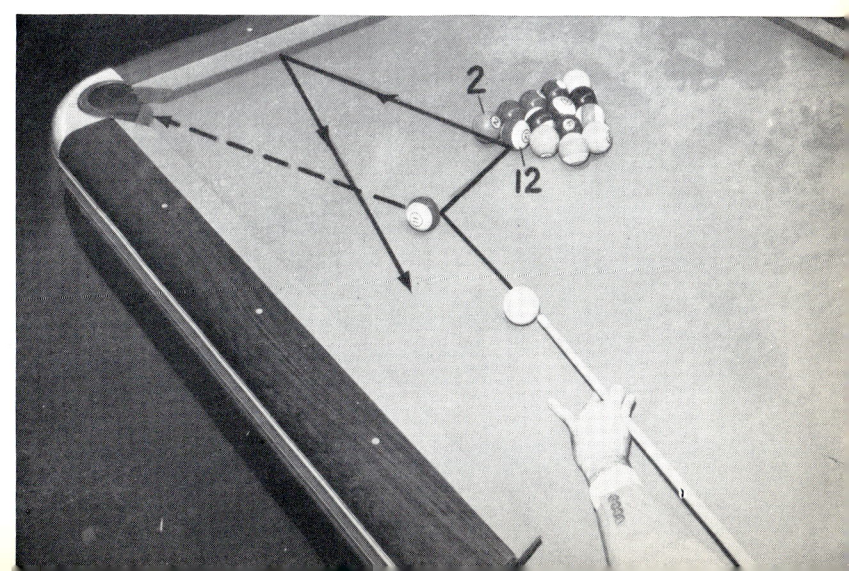

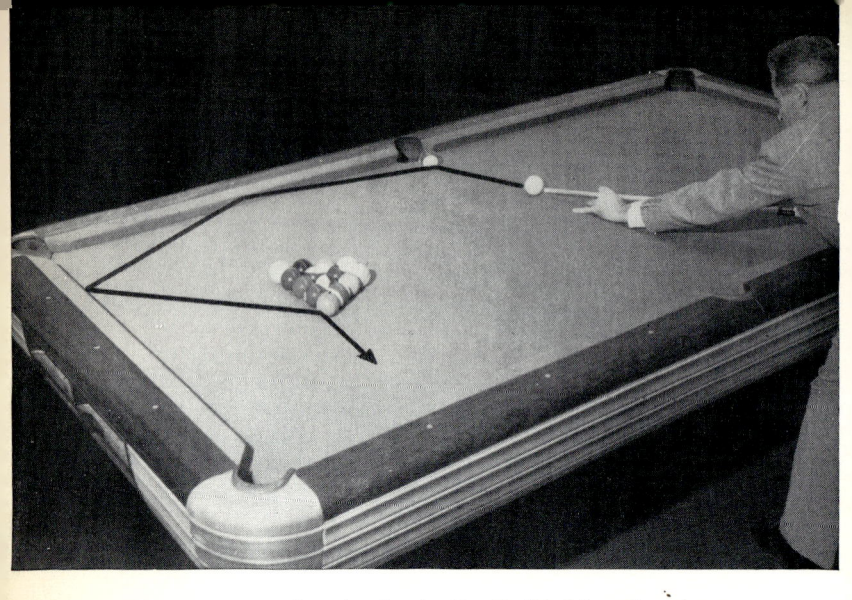

Fig. 91. A side-pocket break. Use English left and stroke cue ball in center of vertical axis. Notice course of cue ball.

Fig. 92. The break ball behind the rack. Use follow on your cue ball, but use no English. Cue ball will move as diagrammed.

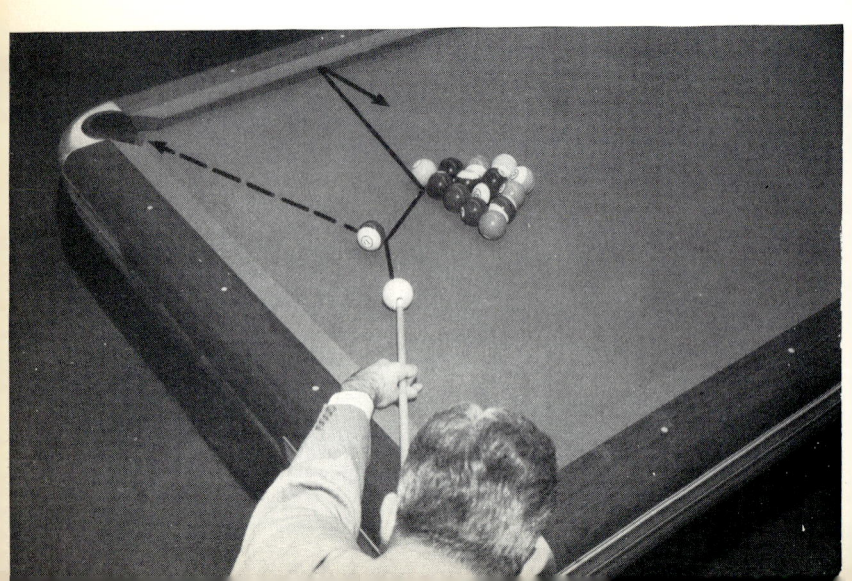

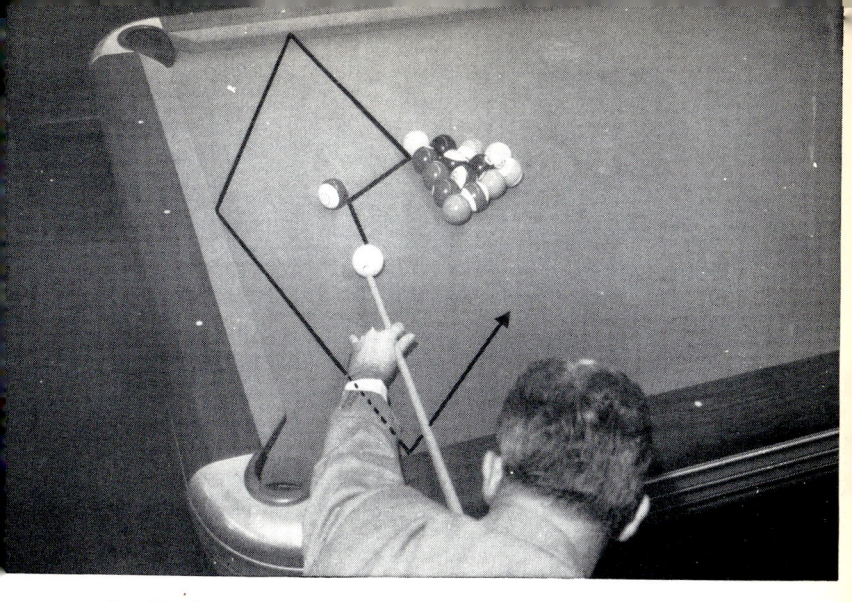

Fig. 93. The cue ball is straighter with the break ball here. Stroke the cue ball slightly above center with English on left.

Fig. 94 Another side-pocket break. Cue the ball in dead center, hold cue level. Cue ball caroms off break ball into the pyramid.

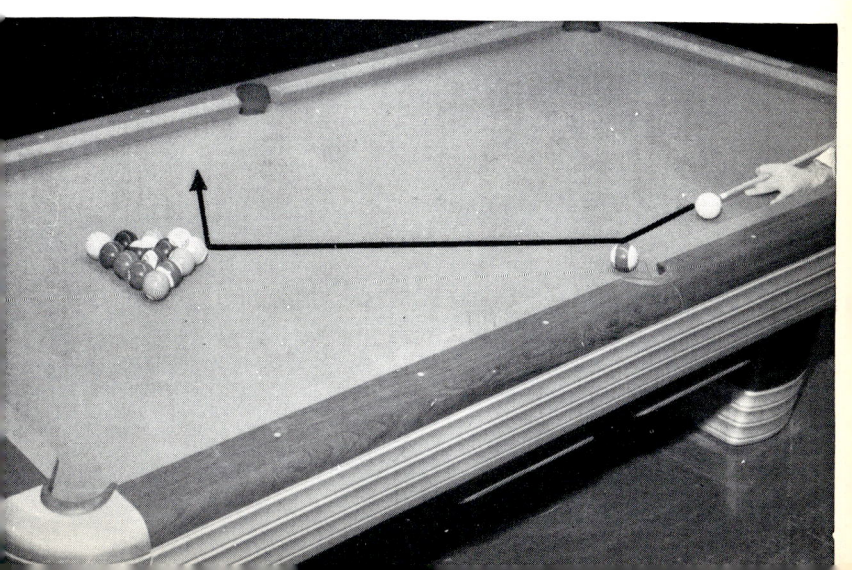

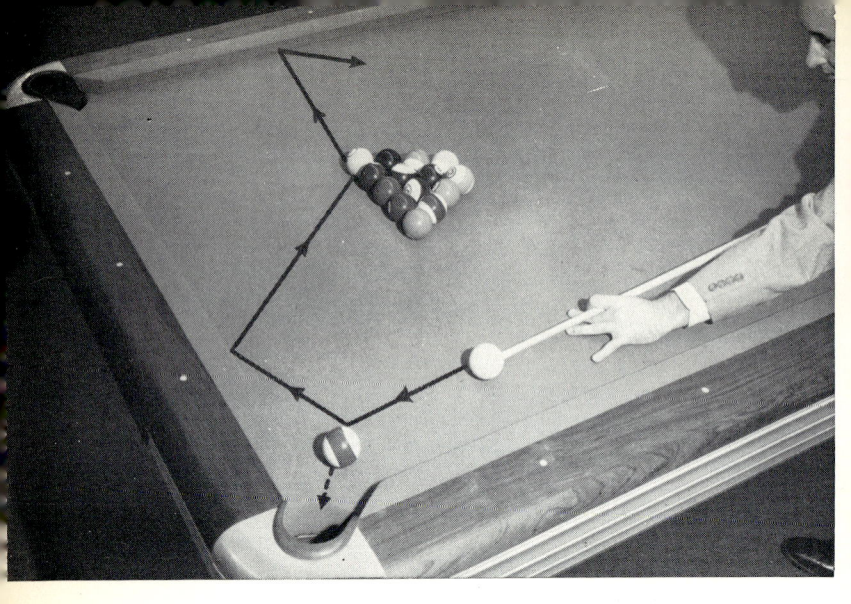

Fig. 95. To make this break shot, you must stroke cue ball with low, right English. The cue ball will roll as indicated above.

Fig. 96. Care must be taken in this break shot to strike object ball at exact point indicated, so cue ball will go to pyramid.

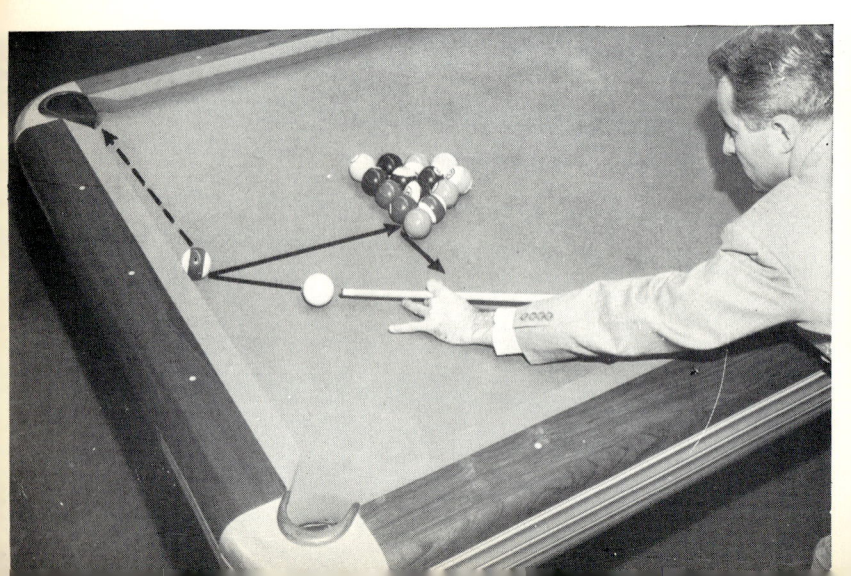

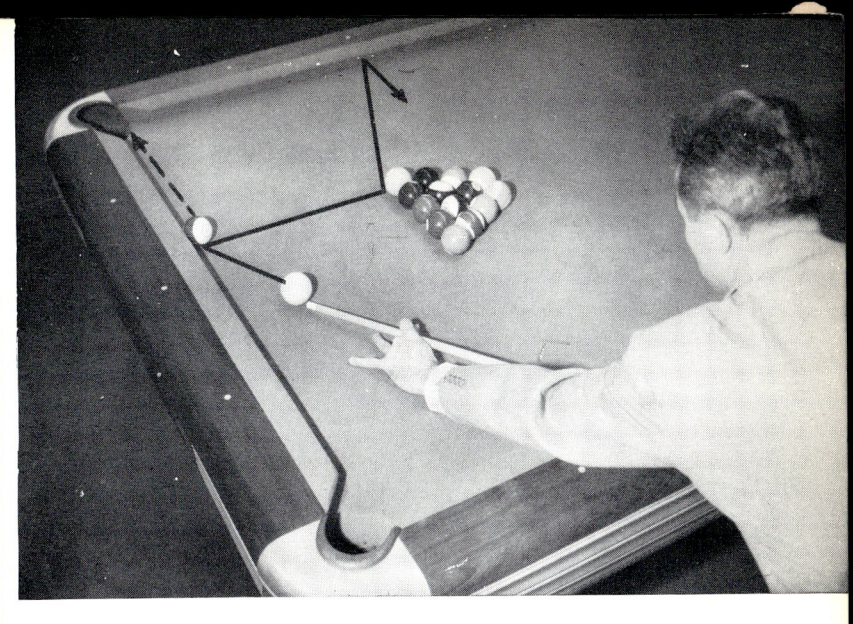

Fig. 97. Use draw stroke and English left for this break shot. Object ball hugs rail to pocket, cue ball draws into rack.

Fig. 98. This shot is made with a follow stroke and English left. Cue ball fights into the rack, spreading the object balls.

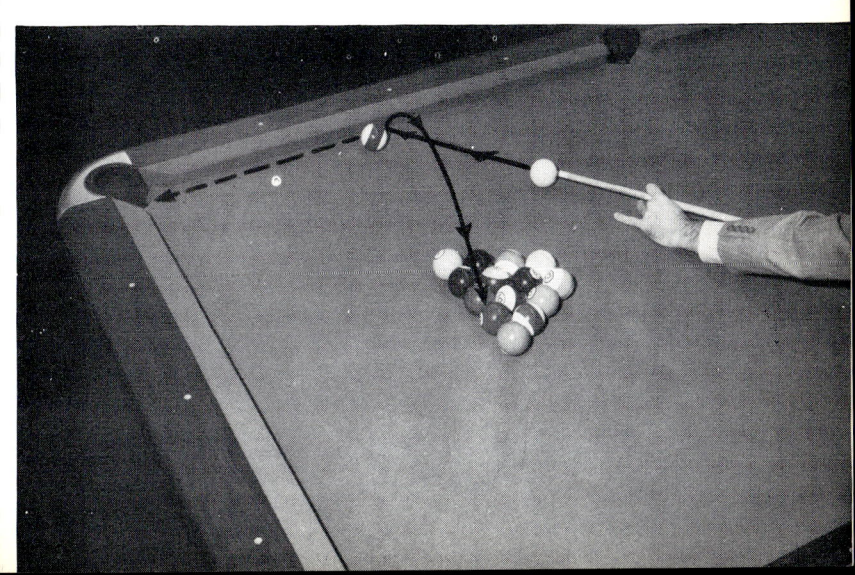

10. Speed of Stroke

WE now have covered about every phase of the championship game of pocket billiards. There is one important item left, however, which no one can teach you. You must learn it yourself. All we can do is to counsel with you, urging you to practice until you have mastered it. That important item is *speed of stroke*. It is, perhaps, the most important phase of good pocket billiard play.

We pointed out earlier that great force is not required in pocket billiards. Rather, the player should develop a soft stroke. Constant practice is the only answer. The player must "feel" the force necessary on the shot that confronts him. Until you develop that "feel" you will have trouble with position play.

We sound alarming on this point because we are trying to stress the importance of speed of stroke. However, any player who has a good stroke, knows how to follow and draw, has mastered the dead-ball stroke, and who *knows the value of center-ball stroking* can, through practice, judge the force necessary.

Speed and Aim

While a judgment of speed is synonymous with position play, it also has an effect on the aim.

We know that English influences the path of the cue

ball to the object ball. We know, too, that English will throw the object ball. We know English adds speed to the cue ball as it caroms from a cushion.

English gets more of an opportunity to work on a soft stroke. Its effect decreases in direct proportion to the velocity of the stroke. You can prove this to yourself by setting up a cut shot for the corner pocket with the cue ball at the other end of the table. (Refer back to Figs. 39 and 40.) If you aim to cut the object ball one-third full and stroke your ball slowly with definite English, the ball will curve enough for you to miss the object ball. If you shoot the same shot at the same point of aim with a hard stroke, the cue ball will curve considerably less.

You can demonstrate the effect of varying speed on the throw of an object ball by setting up a shot about 12 inches out from a side pocket. Place the object ball on a line between the two side pockets. Now place your cue ball on the same line about 12 inches behind the object ball.

With center-ball stroking you would hit the object ball in the exact center to pocket the ball. If employing left English, however, you know the object ball will be thrown to the right. Thus, you aim to the right of center on the object ball as you use right English. If your stroke is soft you will move more to the right of center, because you know English will throw the object ball more on a soft stroke. If you are stroking hard you move less to the right of center on the object ball, since English does not take as effectively on a hard stroke. On an unusually difficult shot, with English, you might have to hit the object ball in the center to pocket it.

It is important to remember, also, that a cue ball

Fig. 99. A good setup for practicing draw and speed of stroke. Problem is to pocket balls successively in the side pocket.

cued with natural English picks up speed as it leaves the cushions. Also, English widens the angle at which the cue ball comes off the cushion. Since the cue ball picks up speed off the cushion, judgment of force is most essential, since the cue ball may roll as much as four or five feet more than you intended if you stroke too hard. Also, if the angle widens off the cushion more than you intended, you may find yourself in trouble. Remember, however, that the angle off the cushion will widen more on a soft stroke than it will on a hard stroke, the English getting more of an opportunity to work.

A good setup with which you can practice speed of stroke is demonstrated in Fig. 99. The object balls are lined in a semicircle in front of the side pocket. With the cue ball in position as indicated, the problem is to pocket the balls successively in the side pocket, going from left to right.

This practice shot will test your ability to draw the cue ball and your ability to draw the cue ball with desired speed.

Refer back to Figs. 85, 86, 87, and 88 for good practice shots on the judgment of speed. Set up shots similar to these for additional practice, placing the square of paper at various positions on the table. You can draw back from an object ball onto the paper; you can follow through the object ball to get on the paper; you can set up shots where you have to go to one or more cushions with follow or draw to get on the paper.

11. Practice and Concentration

THERE is no substitute for practice in the game of pocket billiards. Nor is there any substitute for concentration. The best players in the world will practice from four to five hours a day, after a long layoff from competitive play, to get back in stroke. After they are satisfied they are in stroke, they may keep razor-sharp with less than an hour a day practice. Maybe they are satisfied with their stroke after running two or three frames of balls off the table.

At all world's championship tournament sites, you may know, there is always a practice table, where contestants in the tournament can keep in stroke between championship games.

We don't expect the average pocket billiard player to practice four or five hours a day. If he does, of course, he should improve accordingly. The average player should get most of his practice in competitive play. During a game he will have a chance to practice every phase of the sport.

All players, however, should do some practicing alone — working to improve on their weaknesses. If you are weak on draw shots, work on draw shots, setting up and shooting the same shot over and over again until you have mastered the shot to your satisfaction. Do the same with follow shots, if necessary. Perfect your stop-ball technique. Practice long shots. Practice shots in which you have to drive the object ball a long distance to the pocket.

One of the best ways to "practice" is to watch star players in competitive play. No matter how good you are you can always learn something by watching champions play. Also, the apparent ease with which the champions accomplish what they are trying to do makes the game appear simple. You may be inspired to the conviction "if he can do it, so can I."

Now, lest we leave you with the thought that pocket billiards is simple, let me remind you that, on the contrary, it is a very complicated game, but it becomes easier as your skill improves and your knowledge of the game becomes more extensive.

Concentration

Concentration in pocket billiards means, simply, "Keep your mind on what you are doing." If you are at the billiard table, concentrate on what you are doing. Don't let anything distract your attention.

And, what is just as important, concentrate on what you are supposed to do until that "know how" becomes so much a part of your game that you will do it naturally.

The beginner, for example, must concentrate to make certain that his bridge is firm and solid and comparatively short. He must make sure his grip on the butt end of the cue is light but secure. He must be certain that his stroke is springlike and that he is following through. He must know that his stroke is so grooved that he can strike the cue ball where he intends, even though he is looking at the object ball as he strokes. He must be careful that he is contacting

LITTLE SPORTS LIBRARY

the object ball at the point of aim. And, above all, the beginner should concentrate on center-ball stroking until he has made the above factors a natural part of his game.

The better player must concentrate on speed of stroke and strategy of play, until he can shoot his shots with regard to good position, automatically, and until he can size up at a glance the best way to proceed against the situation which confronts him on the table.

Imagination

Imagination plays its part, too, in this game of pocket billiards, just as it does in any sport. In pocket billiards, the player must have imagination as he sizes up a frame of balls and determines how he will play through the frame, quickly picking out his break ball and the key ball, which will leave him in position on the break ball.

Imagination has a definite place in safety play. The good safety player is the fellow who can think along with his opponent, outsmarting him if possible. Safety play in pocket billiards can be likened to checkers, for example, where the player plans several moves ahead, or, perhaps, to football, in which a sequence of plays is used to catch the other team napping on the pay-off play of the sequence.

12. Conclusion

I believe that in these pages we have provided a comprehensive text on the subject of "How to Play Pocket Billiards." We have told you what to do and how to do it. I am confident that any player — beginner, dub, average player, or star — can improve his game by applying the points covered here. The field, of course, is wide open for the beginner and dub, while the player of average skill will improve in proportion to his natural talent and application.

Not everyone who reads this book is going to develop into a champion. In billiards, as in other sports, champions are born, not made.

But anyone, man, woman, or child, can learn to play better by utilizing this book as a guide.

Remember, pocket billiards is a game. Millions of people play it because it is fun. It is ideal recreation, serving as a mild exercise, and is a wholesome mental "change of pace." The better you and I play the game, the more fun it is.

APPENDIX A
*Glossary of Billiard Terms**

ANGLED. A player is "angled" in pocket billiards and snooker when the corner of a pocket prevents him from shooting the cue ball in a straight line at an object ball.

BALK. The area between the head string and the head of the table. An object ball is in balk, for example, if it lies within the head string when the player has the cue ball in hand. In such cases, object ball in balk is usually spotted on the foot spot, depending on specific game rules.

BALL OFF THE TABLE. Usually a jumped ball; one which after a stroke comes to rest other than on the bed of the table.

BALL ON. A ball is said to be on when a player can shoot directly at it in a straight line.

In snooker a ball is on—that is, a player is said to be "on a ball" — when that ball can be legally struck by the cue ball under the rules.

Also, in pocket billiards a ball may be "on a pocket" if it can be driven into a called pocket on a combination or kiss shot.

BALLS STRUCK SIMULTANEOUSLY. Balls may be struck simultaneously in call-shot pocket billiards if player calls ball and pocket; in other pocket games not requiring a

---
*Reprinted by permission from *The Official Billiards Rule Book*.

_____ MOSCONI ON POCKET BILLIARDS

certain object ball be hit first (rotation), and in snooker, two reds may be struck simultaneously.

BALLS TOUCHING. *See* "Frozen Balls."

BALLS, VALUE OF. The scoring value of balls depends on game stipulations. In rotation pocket billiards, for example, the scoring value of the ball in points corresponds to the number on the ball. A player who scores the 15-ball is credited with 15 points.

BANK SHOT. A bank shot results when a player banks the cue ball or, in pocket billiards, drives an object ball against a cushion (banks it) and then into a pocket from that cushion.

BREAK. In all pocket games, the break is the opening shot of the game, the player being required to "break" the object balls as set forth by the rules of the game being played.

In snooker, a break is a series of consecutive scoring strokes in one turn (inning) at the table. (High run.)

BRIDGE. The placement of the left hand (for right-handed players) on the table as it holds and guides the tip-end of the cue in stroking.

Also, a cuelike stick with a notched plate at the tip end, which a player may use as a "bridge" in shooting over a ball or in making a shot he cannot otherwise reach.

BUST. A bust is a term used in 41-pocket billiards. Player "busts" when he scores more than 41 points and, as a result, must start over with no points.

CALL SHOT. A requirement in some pocket games which insists that a player make known his scoring intentions and then abide by his declaration. In other words, the player must call the ball he intends to make and the pocket in which he intends to drop the ball. If he fails, it is a miss.

CALLED BALL. In pocket games, the ball a player announces he intends to score in a called pocket.

CALLED POCKET. The pocket into which a player announces he intends to drop a called ball.

CAROM. A carom in billiards is a score or a count, the result of the cue ball bounding from one object ball to another. A carom may be made by the cue ball glancing off one object ball directly into the second (or third) object, or by glancing off first object ball into a cushion and then into the second (or third) object.

CENTER SPOT. A spot in the exact center of the table on which a cue ball or an object ball may be spotted in games requiring the use of that spot.

COUNT. A count is a score — a point or a number of points, depending on the game. In most games of pocket billiards, for example, a count or score is one point. In rotation pocket billiards, a count is a score in which the scoring player gets points corresponding to the number of the ball.

CUE BALL IN HAND. A player has a cue ball in hand when, as the result of a foul or error on the part of his opponent, or as the result of some other governing situation, he puts the ball in play at a point of his choice within the head string. (*See Appendix B.*)

CUSHION. A cushion is the cloth-covered resilient ridge which borders the inside of the rails on carom and pocket billiard tables.

DEAD BALL. A dead ball is one that stops or rolls "dead" upon contact with an object. A cue ball, for example, which stops upon contacting an object ball is called a "dead ball."

DEAD BALL SHOT. A shot in which the cue ball becomes "dead" upon contacting an object ball.

DRAW. A stroking technique which allows the player to draw the cue ball back from an object ball.

DRAW SHOT. A shot in which the player applies draw to the stroked cue ball.

ENGLISH. Stroking influence a player is able to put on a cue ball to control the action of that ball either after or before it hits an object ball. Sometimes referred to as spin.

FANCY SHOT. Usually an exhibition shot; a shot that requires unusual skill on the part of the player; a trick shot.

FEATHERING. To feather an object ball is to hit it very thin.

FOLLOW. A stroking technique which allows the player to make the cue ball "follow" in the same general direction as the object ball after it strikes an object ball. Opposed to "draw."

FOLLOW SHOT. One in which the player has applied "follow" to the cue ball.

FOLLOW-THROUGH. A most important fundamental in stroking the cue ball; follow movement of the cue after contact with the cue ball, through the area occupied by cue ball before it was struck by cue. As opposed to checking or jerking cue back after it strikes cue ball.

FORCE. The amount of force applied to the cue ball by the player. An understanding of force required on certain shots adds to the player's skill.

FORCE DRAW. The powerful application of "draw" to the cue ball. Force draw may "force" the cue ball "through" the object ball before the cue ball begins to draw back, or its application may draw the cue ball a great distance back from the object ball.

FORCE FOLLOW. The application of follow in which the player, when "straight" on an object ball, may drive the cue ball in a straight line "through" the object ball, thus attaining desired position.

FOOT SPOT. A spot near the foot of the table at the point where lines drawn from the center diamonds on the short rails and from the second diamonds on the long rails (near foot of table) intersect. The spot for the placement of object balls at the start of most billiard games.

FOOT OF TABLE. The short rail of a billiard or pocket table which is not marked with the manufacturer's name plate. As opposed to the "head of the table," which is marked with the manufacturer's name plate.

FOUL. Any infraction of the rules governing billiards. Fouls are usually penalized by the loss of points, the penalty depending upon specific game rules.

FOUL STROKE. An infraction of the rules in which the foul takes place as a result of the player's stroke. Pushing the cue ball is a foul stroke in most games. Double contact of the cue tip on the cue ball (two separate contacts) is a foul stroke.

FROZEN. A term used to describe balls that are touching each other on the table. When object balls are frozen they remain in play as they are. When cue ball is frozen to an object ball, player proceeds according to the rules of the game being played.

A ball, too, may be frozen to a cushion, that is, resting against the cushion.

FULL BALL. A term used to define contact of a cue ball on an object ball. Some shots in pocket billiards, for example, require that cue ball strike object ball full — that is, in exact center. As opposed to half-ball, one-third ball, one-quarter ball, etc.

GAME. A name for billiards in general and for specific phases of the general game, as pocket billiard game; three-cushion game, etc.

Also, a victory. For example, a player has "game" if he wins.

HEAD OF TABLE. The short rail marked by the manufacturer's name plate. As opposed to foot of table, not marked by manufacturer's name plate.

HEAD SPOT. A spot on the table near the head at the point where lines drawn from the center diamonds on the

MOSCONI ON POCKET BILLIARDS

short rails and the second diamonds (near head of table) on the side rails intersect.

HEAD STRING. A line which, drawn from the second diamonds on the side rails (near the head of the table), runs through the head spot. The area between the head string and the head of the table is referred to as "within the head string," or as a "balk."

HOLD. Usually reverse English. The application of English to a cue ball which tends to hold the cue ball back from the course the ball normally would take, having been driven in a certain direction.

HUG THE RAIL. Used to define the action of a cue ball which, because of "hold English," tends to stay close to a rail. Application of English may cause ball to roll along rail or cause it to bounce against the same rail one or more times as it travels along that rail.

INNING. A turn at the table. The duration of a player's stay at the table from the time he legally makes the first shot of a turn until he ends his turn, either by missing, fouling, scoring the maximum number of balls allowed, or terminating the game.

KISS. A kiss is a carom. The cue ball may kiss from one object ball to another. An object ball, already struck by the cue ball, may kiss the second object ball either into or from the path of the cue ball. In pocket games, the cue ball may kiss from one object ball into another to score the latter ball.

HIGH RUN. The highest consecutive series of scores in one inning of a game or of a tournament.

LAGGING. A procedure resorted to by players to determine rotation of play.

LINE-UP. A pocket billiard game. Also, method of spotting balls in game of line-up.

LIVE BALL. A ball which is in play under the rules. Also, the cue ball, when its action is "alive," as opposed to a "dead ball."

LONG STRING. An imaginary line running from the foot spot to the center of the foot rail, on which balls are spotted in pocket billiard games, when the foot spot is occupied or when more than one object ball must be spotted. (*See* Rotation Pocket Billiards, *Appendix B.*) Long string line is also extended beyond the foot spot for the placement of spotted balls, if the line between the foot spot and the foot of the table is totally occupied.

MASSE. Extreme application of English on a cue ball, applied by elevating the cue.

MASSE SHOT. A shot in which the player uses massé.

MISCUE. Faulty stroke; faulty contact of the tip of the cue against the cue ball. A stroke in which the cue tip slips from the cue ball, not applying action as planned, due to a defective tip, improper chalking of cue tip and, in many instances, to excessive English.

MISS. Failure on the part of a player to accomplish his intention on a stroke. A miss may or may not be a foul, depending upon rules of game being played.

NATURAL. A simple shot; one which can be made directly (in pockets) or as the result of a simple angle in carom billiards; a shot with a natural angle, as opposed to a shot that is "not on."

PUSH SHOT. Shoving or pushing cue ball with the tip of the cue; also two contacts of the cue tip on cue ball. Push shots are legal in pockets if stroke is made with what appears to be one continuous (uninterrupted) motion of the cue. Referee is sole judge as to whether a player was guilty of an illegal push shot in pockets.

PYRAMID. The placement of the object balls in pocket games when the balls are racked in a triangle at the foot spot to start the game.

RACK. The wooden triangle used to pyramid balls at the foot spot for the opening shot in pocket billiard games.

Also, the grouping of the balls at the foot spot in pyramid formation after the wooden triangle has been removed.

MOSCONI ON POCKET BILLIARDS

For example, the player, on the opening shot, drives the cue ball into the rack (into the racked balls).

RAIL. The flat surfaces of the table, above the table bed, from which the cushions slope. There are two end rails and two side rails. The rail marked with the manufacturer's name plate is the head rail. The unmarked short rail is the foot rail. The rail to the right, standing at the head and facing the foot, is the right rail. The other long rail is the left rail.

REVERSE. English applied to put "hold" on the ball. (*See* "Hold.")

ROTATION. The name of a pocket game in which player must drive cue ball against object balls in numerical order.

Also, the sequence of play when two or more players are involved, as "rotation of play."

RUN. A series of consecutive scores or counts in one inning.

SAFETY. A defense measure a player can resort to when confronted with a difficult shot. He sacrifices an opportunity to score, as well as his turn at the table, in an attempt to leave a difficult shot for his opponent.

SCRATCH. Generally an unanticipated development as the result of a player's stroke, which may or may not be a foul, depending upon the situation and rules of the game. A player may "scratch" the cue ball into a pocket; he may "scratch" a point as the result of a kiss, which point otherwise he would not have made, etc.

SETUP. An easy shot.

SNOOKERED. To be the victim of a snooker; to be unable to shoot the cue ball in a direct line at the object ball which is on.

SPOT. *See* head, foot, center spots, spot shot, spot ball, spotting balls.

SPOT BALL. A ball which is placed on the foot, head, or center spot at the start of a game, or after having been illegally pocketed or forced off the table, or which is spotted

113

as the result of a specific game requirement, as when 15th-ball interferes with racking in 14-1 continuous pocket billiards.

SPOT SHOT. A shot in which the player shoots at a ball that has been placed on a spot. The opening shot in all carom games is a spot shot.

SPOTTING. The replacement of balls on the table as required by rules of the game. (*See specific games, particularly* Rotation, *in Appendix B.*)

STOP SHOT. A shot in which the cue ball stops on contact with an object ball.

APPENDIX B

Pocket Billiard Games*

General Rules

The general rules of billiards apply in pocket billiards. Since, however, there may be questions as to interpretations of the rules, they are discussed specifically in the following games.

All pocket billiard games are played on a rectangular table twice as long as it is wide. The table may be 4 x 8 feet, 4½ x 9 feet, or 5 x 10 feet. (*See* Diagram 1.)

Simple Pocket Billiards

This game is played with 15 object balls, numbered from 1 to 15, and a white cue ball. The object balls are racked on the foot spot. Starting player has cue ball in hand. (*See* Diagram 2.)

Purpose of game: The game can be played by individuals or sides. One individual or side seeks to pocket 8 balls before the opponents. The side pocketing 8 (of the 15) balls first wins.

Start of play: Start of play can be determined by lagging or lot. With cue ball in hand, starting player must pocket a ball, or drive two object balls to a cushion. In nontitle play, incoming player can accept balls in position, if opponent fails to comply with rules for opening shot. In match or tournament play, starting player must pocket a ball or drive two object balls to a cushion. If he fails, opponent can accept balls in position or insist that balls

---
*Reprinted by permission from *The Official Billiards Rule Book*.

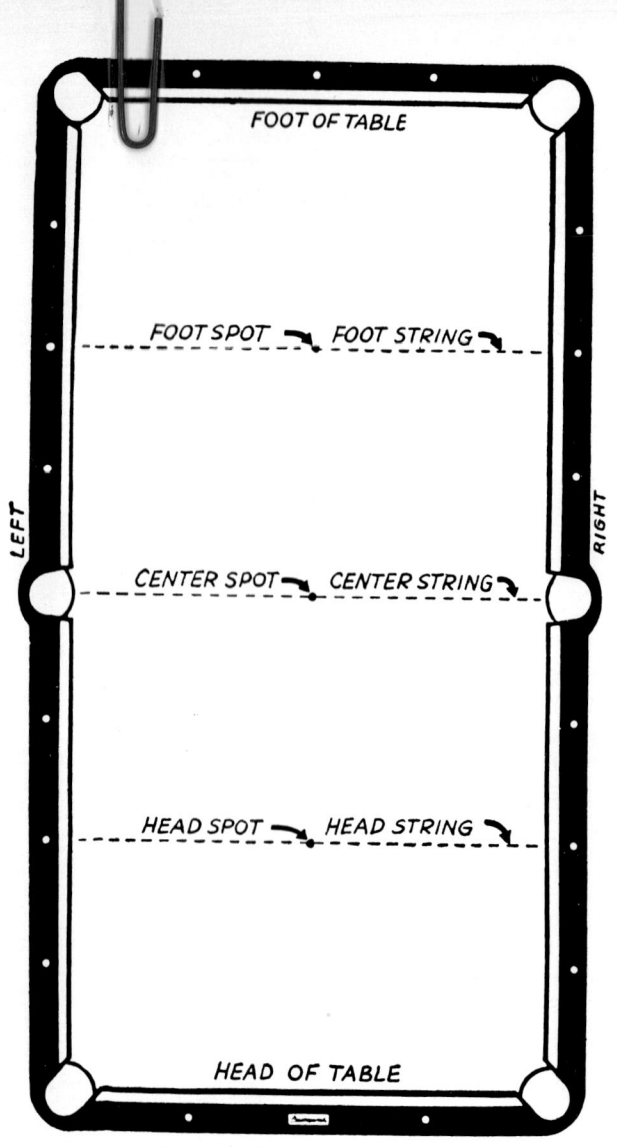

Diagram 1. Pocket billiard table, with locations indicated.

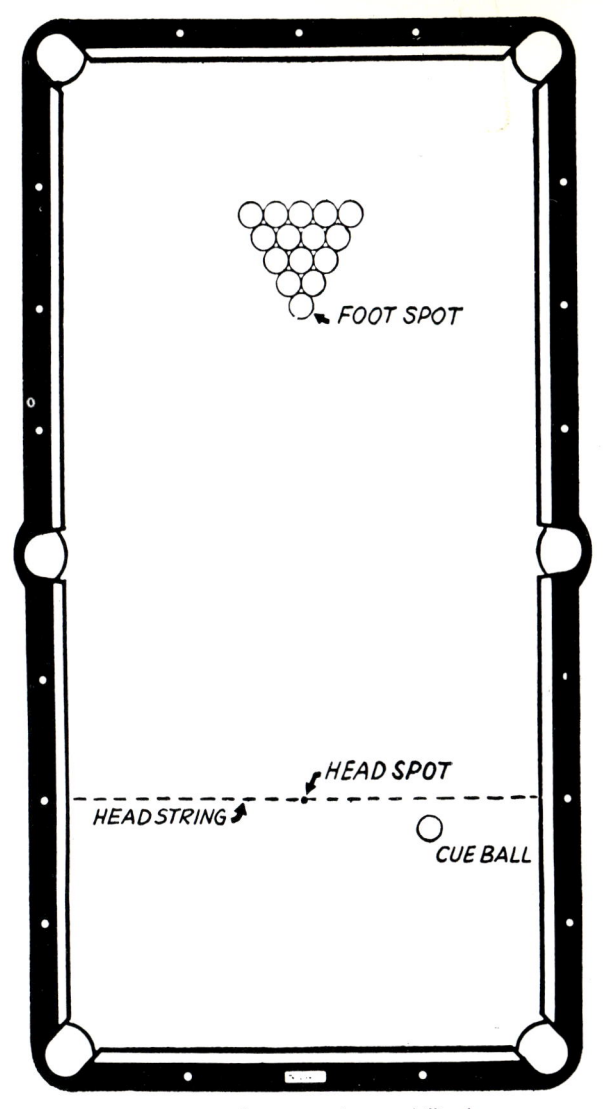

Diagram 2. Setup for start of most billiard games.

be reracked and that opening player continue to break until he complies with the rules. Player does not have to "call his shot" on opening stroke and is credited with all balls legally pocketed.

Subsequent play: On all strokes following the opening shot, the player must call the ball or balls he intends to pocket, although he is not compelled to call the pocket.

If a ball is called, but not pocketed, other balls scored on the stroke do not count. They must be spotted. The player loses his turn at the table but is not penalized.

If a player calls more than one ball, he must pocket all balls called. If he fails, no ball is counted. If balls were pocketed, they are spotted. Player loses turn, but is not penalized.

Failure to hit a called ball is not an error, provided the cue ball touches another object ball.

If a player calls but one ball, which he pockets, he is entitled to all other balls pocketed on the same stroke.

After the opening stroke, the player must either pocket a called ball, drive an object ball to a cushion, or cause the cue ball to contact a cushion after hitting object ball.

Penalties: Penalties are imposed by compelling the offending player to forfeit one ball, in addition to those pocketed on the foul stroke. If a player has no balls to his credit at the time of foul, he owes one to the table, which he must spot when he scores.

If a player fouls twice on the same stroke (such as failing to drive two object balls to the cushion on the break shot and scratching the cue ball in a pocket) only one penalty is imposed.

Player forfeits one point for:

1. Failing to comply with break shot requirements (losing one point more for each successive failure on break).
2. Scratching the cue ball in a pocket.
3. Forcing the cue ball off the table.
4. Shooting while balls are in motion.
5. Failing (after the opening stroke) to pocket a ball, cause

an object ball to hit a cushion, or cause cue ball to hit cushion, after hitting object ball which is not driven to a cushion.
6. Striking cue ball twice on same stroke.
7. Touching cue ball or object balls with hands, cue, clothing, etc., except as on a legal stroke with cue.

Spotting balls: Balls are spotted as outlined in general rules for spotting balls *(See* Rotation).

Interference: If the balls are unlawfully interfered with in any way by the player at the table, incoming player can accept them in position or insist that original position of balls be restored.

If nonplayer interferes with balls, while his opponent is shooting, the offending player loses the game.

If balls are disturbed by any person or influence other than the players, conditions prior to disturbance are restored. Player at table continues his inning.

General rules: Unless covered specifically above, general rules for billiards apply.

Fifteen-Ball Pocket Billiards

The game: The game is played with a cue ball and fifteen object balls. The object balls are racked in the triangle **at** the foot spot. The 15-ball is placed at the apex of the triangle at the foot spot. The next-highest numbered balls are placed near the 15-ball, with the low-numbered balls at the back of the rack. Starting player has cue ball in hand. *(See* Diagram 3.)

Break: Start of play can be determined by lag or lot. With cue ball in hand, the starting player breaks the triangle, being required to pocket a ball or drive at least two object balls to a cushion. He does not have to call his shot.

Scoring: The purpose of the game is to score 61 points first. Players are credited with points corresponding to the numbers on the balls. Thus, if a player pockets the 15-ball, he is credited with 15 points. After the opening

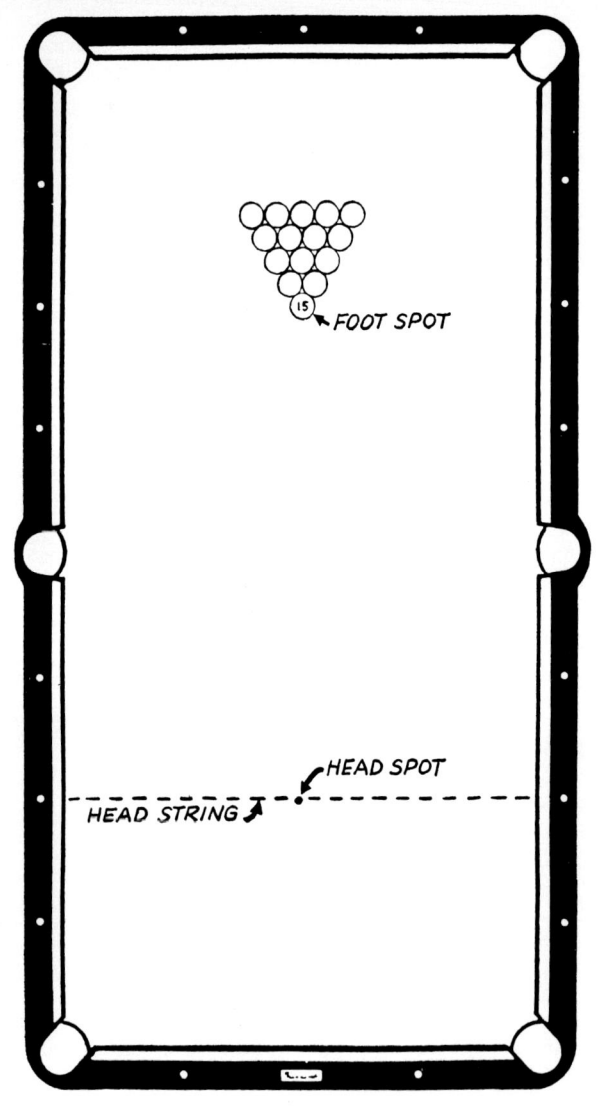

Diagram 3. Table setup for "15-ball" pocket billiard game.

stroke of the game, players must pocket a ball, drive an object ball to a cushion, or cause the cue ball to contact a cushion after hitting an object ball. All balls made on one legal stroke are credited to the player pocketing them. Players are not compelled to call their shots.

Penalties: On the break shot, if the starting player fails to pocket a ball or cause two object balls to go to a cushion, he loses three points, and, under option of his opponent, can be required to break the balls again. If he fails on the second break shot to pocket a ball or cause two object balls to contact a cushion, he forfeits three more points. He loses three points for each successive failure.

A player also forfeits three points if:

A. The cue ball is pocketed.
B. A ball is not pocketed and an object ball is not driven to a cushion, or if the cue ball does not contact a cushion after hitting an object ball which fails to go to a cushion.
C. He forces his cue ball off the table.
D. He shoots out of turn and is detected before he pockets a ball. (If error is not detected and player scores, he continues shooting.)
E. He interferes with the cue ball after a stroke.
F. He strokes when any ball is in motion or spinning.
G. He fails to have one foot on the floor when stroking.

If a player is guilty of one or more fouls on the same stroke (such as failing to drive an object ball to a cushion and causing the cue ball to go into a pocket at the same time) he is penalized only for one foul and loses only three points.

Tie games can be regarded as void and played over, or by arrangement the contestants can spot the 15-ball on the foot spot, lag for the next shot and reopen play with the cue ball in hand. The player scoring the 15 ball wins.

General rules: Unless otherwise covered above, the general rules for 14.1 continuous billiards apply.

Rotation

The game: Rotation pocket billiards is played with a cue ball and 15 object balls, numbered from 1 to 15. The object balls are racked in a triangle at the foot spot. The 1-ball is at the apex of the triangle on the foot spot. The 2-ball is placed at the left apex of the triangle and the 3-ball is placed at the right apex of the triangle. (*See* Diagram 4.)

Break: Order of play may be determined by lagging or lot. Player making first or break shot has cue ball in hand. Opening player is compelled to make the 1-ball the first object ball. If he fails to contact the 1-ball first on the break shot, it is an error and ends his inning. Balls pocketed (if any) on shot are spotted. Incoming player accepts balls in position. The 1-ball is first object.

Scoring: Players must pocket balls in numerical order. Player or side scoring 61 points first wins game. The 1-ball is the first object ball until it is legally pocketed. The 2-ball then becomes the legal object ball; then the 3-ball; then the 4-ball, etc. Rules of the game require that the cue ball must strike legal object ball before touching another ball. Failure is a miss and ends the inning. Balls pocketed on an illegal contact are spotted.

If a player makes a legal contact on the object ball he is entitled to all balls pocketed on that stroke, whether or not he pocketed legal object ball. For example, if a player contacted the 1-ball, which failed to fall into a pocket, but pocketed the 15-ball or some other ball as the result of a combination or a carom, he is entitled to the ball or balls pocketed and continues play, the 1-ball remaining as the object ball.

The lowest numbered ball on the table is the object ball.

Pocketing cue ball: If the cue ball is pocketed it is a scratch and ends the inning. Balls pocketed on stroke are spotted.

Spotting balls: Balls pocketed illegally are spotted on the long string, running from the foot spot to the center

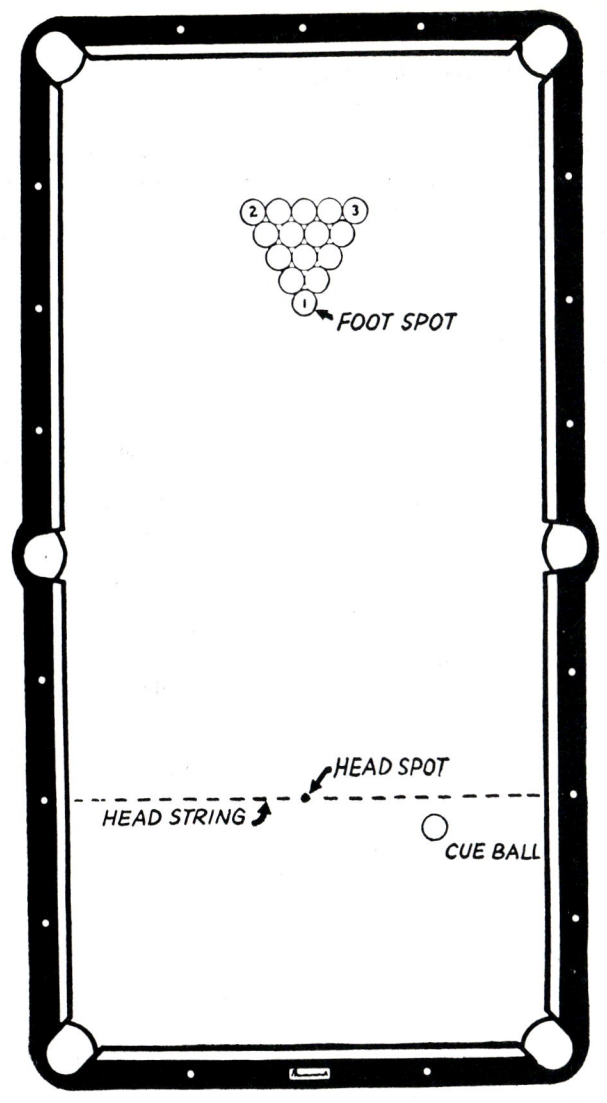

Diagram 4. In rotation game, balls are pocketed in numerical order.

of the foot rail. (*See* Diagram 5.) Balls are spotted in numerical order. For example, if the 1- and 3-balls are illegally pocketed, the 1-ball is placed on the foot spot and the 3-ball is frozen behind it on the string. If the foot spot is occupied, the spotted balls are placed on the long string as close as possible to the spot, also in numerical order. In no case is an object ball or the cue ball resting on the long string moved to make way for a ball to be spotted. Spotted balls are placed either in front or behind such object balls on the long string.

If the long string (between the foot spot and the foot rail) is totally occupied, the balls to be spotted are placed in front of the foot spot, as close as possible to the spot. (*See* Diagram 5.)

If the cue ball rests on the long string, thus interfering with the placement of an object ball, the object ball is placed either in front of or behind the cue ball, as near as possible to the cue ball (which means frozen to the cue ball).

Jumped balls: If one or more object balls jump the table they are spotted. If player contacted legal object ball first and then caused one or more object balls to jump the table, he continues play and is credited with object balls (if any) pocketed on the stroke. If he failed to count, it is a miss and ends his inning.

If the cue ball jumps the table, it is an error and ends the inning. Balls pocketed on stroke are spotted. Incoming player proceeds with cue ball in hand.

Balls within head string: In rotation, if legal object lies between head string and the head of the table, and the striker has the cue ball in hand, the legal object ball is placed on the long string.

Eight Ball

The Game: The game is played with a cue ball and 15 object balls, numbered from 1 to 15. Balls are racked at foot spot, 8-ball in center of triangle. (*See* Diagram 6.)

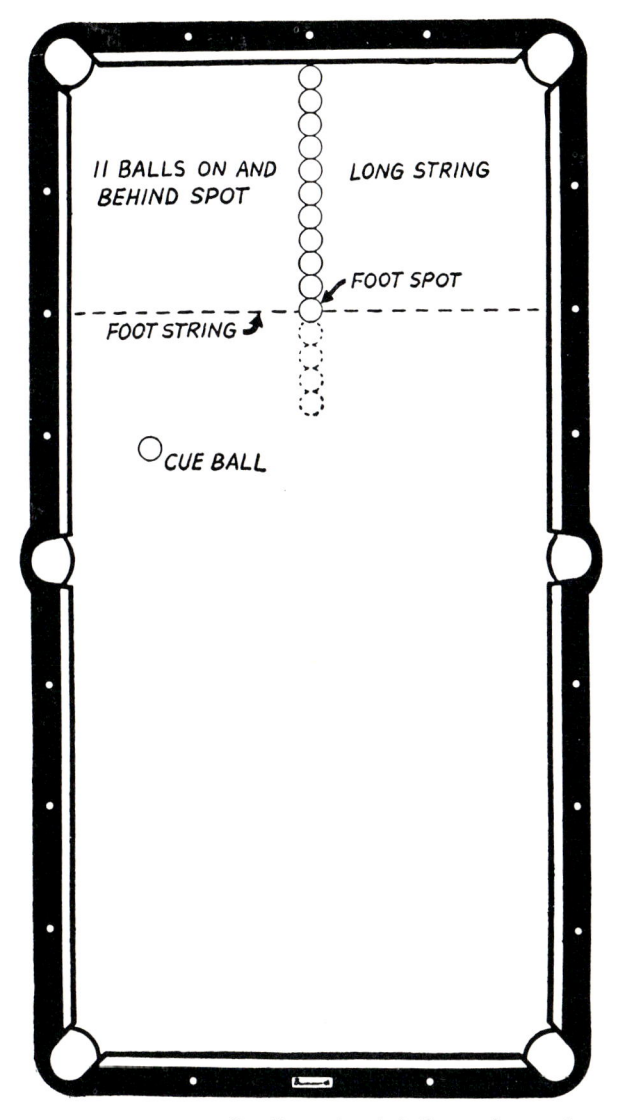

Diagram 5. Spot illegally pocketed balls on long string.

LITTLE SPORTS LIBRARY

One player or side must pocket balls numbered from 1 to 7 or from 9 to 15. Opponent pockets groups of balls not selected by player with original choice. For example, if the player with the first choice chooses to score balls from 1 to 7, the opponent must pocket balls from 9 to 15.

Player or side pocketing numerical group first and then legally pocketing 8-ball wins the game.

Break: Order of play can be determined by lagging or lot. Starting player is not compelled to make a choice on opening shot, nor must he call his shot on the break. If opening player pockets one or more balls on the break, he has his choice of the high or low group. If the breaker fails to pocket a ball on the break, the incoming player accepts balls in position and has his choice of the high or low balls.

Scoring: The striker is entitled to all balls legally pocketed, unless he pockets a ball belonging to his opponent, in which case the opponent is credited with that ball. If player pockets only an opponent's ball and none of his own group, it is a miss.

Combination shots are allowed at all times, except in an attempt to pocket the 8-ball. Player may play combination off opponent's ball.

The rules of Eight Ball specify that the player pocketing the high numerical group of balls must pocket the 15-ball in the left side pocket, that is, in the side pocket to his left as he stands at the head of the table facing the foot of the table.

The player scoring the low-numbered balls must pocket the 1-ball in the right side pocket. If the 1- and 15-balls are not placed in these pockets as required by the rules, they are spotted and respotted until the player is successful in accomplishing this purpose.

After a player has pocketed all the balls in his numerical group, he shoots to pocket the 8-ball, calling his shot. If shooting directly at the 8-ball (not banking), the player

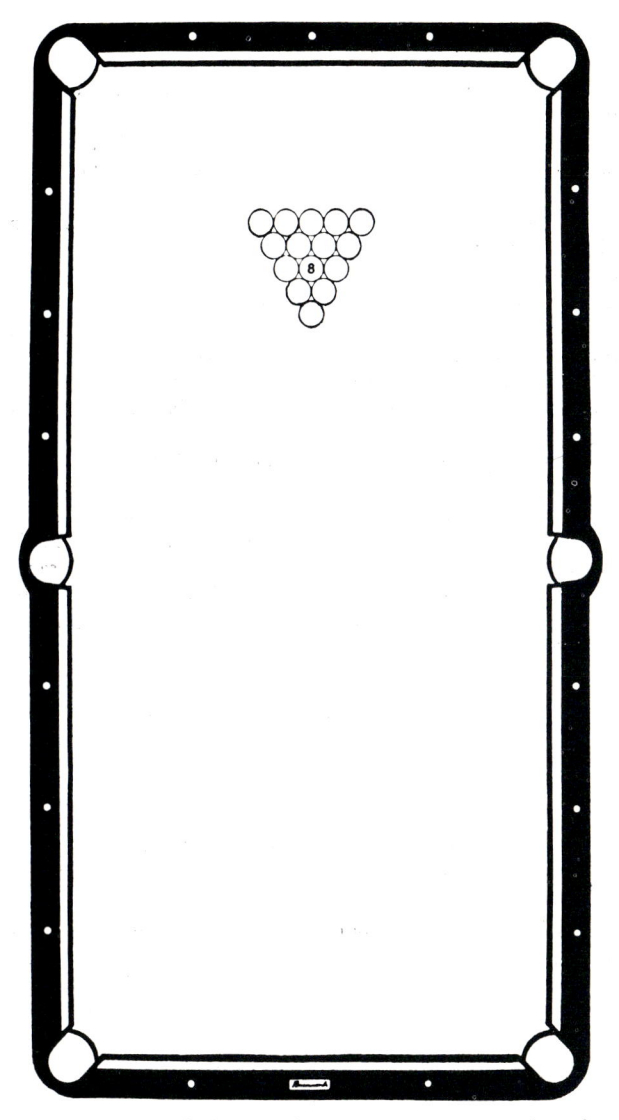

Diagram 6. Eight ball. The 8-ball is in center of triangle rack.

must pocket that ball or cause the 8-ball or the cue ball to contact a cushion.

Loss of game: If the player, shooting directly at the 8-ball, fails to cause the cue ball to go to a cushion after hitting 8-ball, or the 8-ball to contact a cushion, he loses the game. If banking 8-ball, players must hit the 8-ball. If a player accidentally pockets the 8-ball before he pockets all the balls of his numerical group, he loses the game.

When playing for the 8-ball, player must hit that ball first. If he pockets the 8-ball on a combination, he loses the game. If he fails to hit 8-ball on bank, he loses game.

Since a player is required to call his shot when playing for the 8-ball, he loses the game if the 8-ball drops into a pocket not designated on the call.

When if player is shooting to make the 8-ball, he loses the game if cue ball scratches in pocket.

Within the string: When player has cue ball in hand and object balls rest within the head string, the object ball nearest to the string is spotted on the foot spot. The same is done when the 8-ball is the object ball and lies within the head string and the player has the cue ball in hand.

Championship Game

The game of 14.1 continuous pocket billiards is the game of champions — the game in which title honors in pocket billiards are decided. It is the ideal competitive game, requiring that a player have an all-around pocket billiard-playing skill.

The following rules for tournament play were adopted prior to the 1948 world's championship and are still in force.

The Game: Fourteen-one continuous pocket billiards is played with a cue ball and fifteen object balls, numbered from 1 to 15. Tournament play pits individual against individual, but the game could be played by partners or by teams.

Break: Contending players lag for the break. Winner

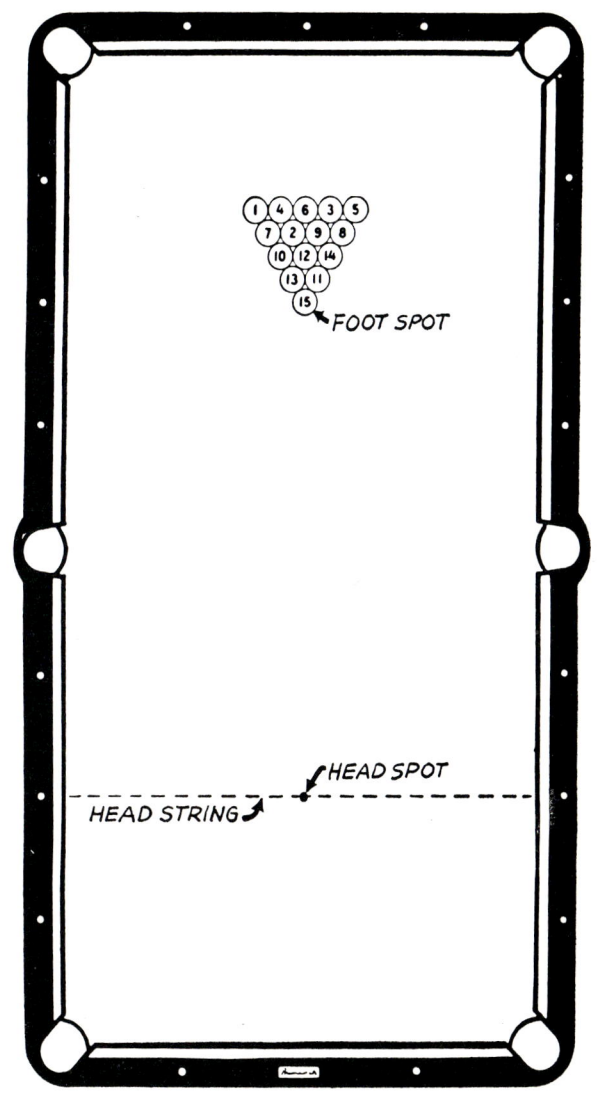

Diagram 7. Note opening placement in continuous 14.1 game.

of lag has option of assigning break to his opponent, which usually happens on account of the improbability of pocketing a designated ball on the break shot.

Rack: Balls are racked in a triangle at the foot of the table. The 15-ball is placed in the apex of the triangle on the foot spot. The 1-ball is placed in the left apex of the triangle and the 5-ball is placed at the right apex. The highest-numbered balls should be placed near the foot spot apex of the triangle, the lowest-numbered balls near the base of the triangle. (*See* Diagram 7.)

Before a tournament or championship match opens, the referee must draw a pencil line from the foot spot to the exact center of the foot rail, thus assuring continuous accuracy in spotting the balls.

Referee must also draw a pencil line on the cloth around the triangle after he places it for opening of game, this, also, assuring accurate placement of the triangle for subsequent break shots.

Requirements of break: Starting player has cue ball in hand for break shot. Starting player, on the opening stroke, must drive two or more object balls to a cushion or cause an object ball to drop in a pocket. (If he drops a ball in a pocket, he does not get credit for that ball unless he called his shot.)

If the starting player fails to comply with the requirements of the break, the stroke is foul, he loses two points and, at the option of his opponent, may lose his inning, or, with the balls reframed, may be compelled by his opponent to break again. Opening player loses two points for each successive failure to meet requirements of break.

If, however, opening player drives two balls to a cushion as required and scratches the cue ball into a pocket, he loses his inning, is penalized only one point and the incoming player has the cue ball in hand.

When the opening player legally breaks the object balls, without pocketing a designated ball, the incoming player accepts the balls in position.

Scoring: In championship tournament play, the player scoring 125 points first wins the game.

In championship match play, when the defense of the title depends upon more than one block, the winning block score may be 125 or 150 or any stated number of points agreed upon by the contestants.

If a match block score is 125, the player scoring 125 points first wins the block, but he must continue play until he pockets all the object balls on the table but one.

If a player after having won the block by scoring 125 points, misses in an attempt to clear the table of all object balls but one, the opponent comes to the table, clearing it of all object balls but one; and the player who cleared the table makes the opening shot in the next block.

In subsequent blocks, the player scoring 125 points first wins the block. If, however, the winner of the second block is behind in total points for the match, play continues until one of the players has a total of 250 points, the number required for two blocks. If this situation prevails in the third block, play continues until one player has scored 375 points, and so on.

Call shots: The game of 14.1 continuous pocket billiards is a call-shot game. The player must designate the ball he expects to pocket and the pocket in which he expects to score, making his intention known to the referee, unless it is clearly obvious to the referee what the player intends. In the latter case, the referee calls the object ball. If he errs in his call, the player must correct him before striking the cue ball.

Combination and carom shots are legal in 14.1 pocket billiards.

The player is entitled to one point for every ball called and pocketed. If he pockets the called ball and others in addition on the same stroke, he is credited with one point for each ball pocketed.

Object balls pocketed illegally are spotted on the long string. (*See* "Spotting Balls," Rotation.) (*See* Diagram 5.)

Misses: If the player misses the shot called, it is an error and ends his inning. The striker is not penalized for failing to make the cue ball contact the designated object ball, providing the cue ball hits at least one other object ball, driving this latter object ball to a cushion or into a pocket, or providing the cue ball hits a cushion after hitting an object ball. If the player, however, misses the designated object ball and fails to contact another object ball, driving the latter to a cushion or into a pocket, or if he fails to cause the cue ball to hit a cushion after it hits an object ball that isn't driven to a cushion, it is a foul, ends the inning and the player loses one point.

Continuous play: In 14.1 continuous pocket billiards, a player may pocket 14 balls successively. The 15th ball remains on the table as a break ball. The referee then racks the 14 pocketed balls, leaving the space at the foot spot vacant in the triangle. (*See* Diagram 8.) A second cue ball may be placed as the 15th ball in the foot spot apex of the triangle to assure accurate framing of the balls and then removed after the rack is taken off the balls.

Player then continues, making the ball outside the triangle the break ball. His procedure is to pocket the break ball in a designated pocket and carom the cue ball from the break ball into the triangle of racked balls. Player may carom cue ball from break ball into one or more cushions and then into rack. However, player is not compelled to shoot at break ball. He may, if he chooses, strike any ball in rack. (Rules for misses apply.)

If player pockets break ball or calls and pockets shot in rack he continues play. Player can continue counting 14 balls, having them reracked and breaking until he misses, scratches or scores the required number of points for game.

Game ends: A championship tournament game ends when a player scores 125 points. In championship match play, however, when play continues from block to block, player, after counting 125 points, must clear the table of all object balls but the break ball, thus being in a posi-

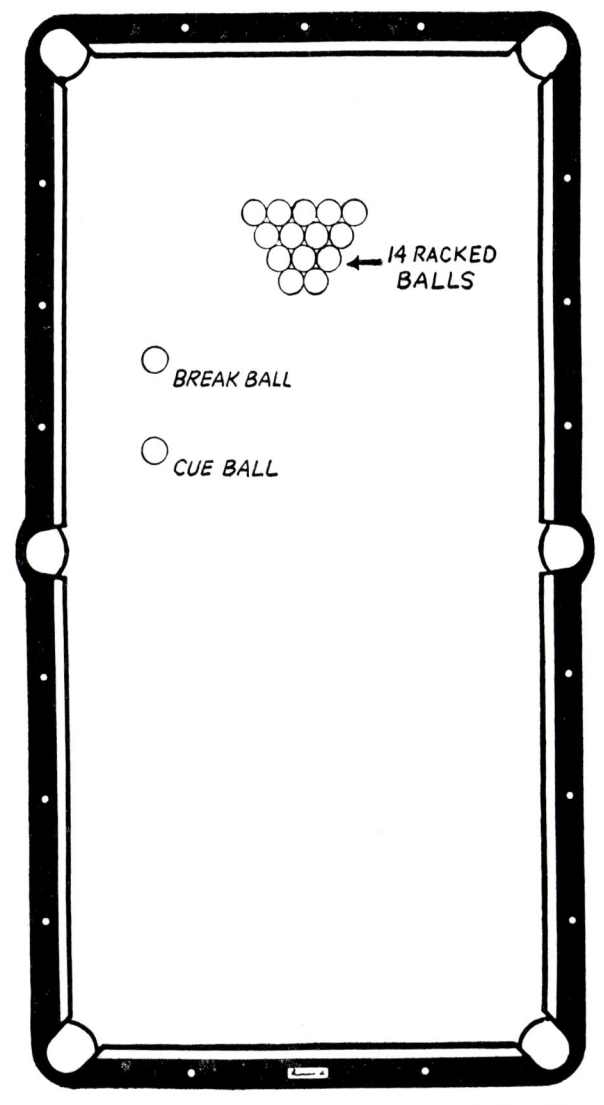

Diagram 8. After run of 14, referee racks balls like this.

tion to continue his run at the opening of the next block. (*See* Scoring, *above*.)

Marking position of balls: At the conclusion of the block in match play, the referee marks the position of the cue ball and the position of the lone object ball with a pencil, indicating the number of the next block. For example, if the players have concluded the sixth block, the referee when marking the position of the cue ball and object ball, places a 7 where each ball rested on the table. Thus, the balls are marked for the opening shot of the seventh block.

Final block: In the final block, play ceases when player pockets the ball that brings his total to the specified number of points to win the match.

Ball frozen to a cushion. When an object ball is frozen to a cushion or within two inches of the cushion (in the referee's judgment), player can play safety off that ball; but to play a legal safety, he must pocket the object ball, drive the object ball to another cushion, or cause the cue ball to contact another cushion after striking object ball. If he fails to comply with above stipulations, player fouls and loses one point.

If in doubt as to the distance of the ball from the cushion, player, attempting a safety, can ask the referee for a ruling. If the ball is within two inches of the cushion, referee will say "in," which compels the player to proceed as stated above. If the ball, according to the referee, is not within two inches of the cushion, referee will say "out." Player can then proceed as the general rules permit.

(NOTE: This rule has been approved by the Billiard Congress of America and tournament players to eliminate a possible situation which would permit legal stalling. The rule speeds up the game, making it more attractive from a spectator standpoint. Also, it states definitely the procedure a player must follow, when an object ball is within two inches of the cushion and a player wants to play safe off the ball. Former rules on this subject were indefinite and placed an unnecessary burden on the referee's judgment.)

Cue ball within the string: Since, when the cue ball is in hand, the player must place the cue ball within the head string, he loses his inning and forfeits one point if he shoots after having been warned by the referee that the cue ball is not within the string. Incoming player accepts balls in position or can insist conditions be restored to what they were before opponent fouled. If the cue ball is not within the string and the player shoots and counts before the foul is detected, he receives credit for balls pocketed and continues play. If he misses, it merely ends his inning.

Push shots: A push shot made with one continuous stroke of the cue is legal, whether the cue ball is frozen to an object ball or not. Foul stroke is penalized by loss of one point. The referee is the sole judge in ruling on legality of a push shot.

Frozen cue ball: When the cue ball is in contact with an object ball, player may play directly at object ball in contact with cue ball, provided the object ball is moved and the cue ball strikes a cushion, or provided the object ball which is in contact with the cue ball is driven to a cushion. Failure to comply with this requirement is a foul. Penalty: loss of one point.

Foot on floor: When shooting the player must have one foot touching the floor. Failure is a foul. Penalty: loss of one point.

Interference: If a player, deliberately or accidentally, obstructs, disturbs, or touches in any manner the cue ball or an object ball with the butt or side of his cue, his necktie, coat, his hand or any part of body or clothes, he has fouled. By way of penalty, he loses his inning and forfeits one point from his score.

Balls in motion: A stroke made while the cue ball and/or object balls are in motion or spinning is a foul. Penalty: loss of one point. Incoming player can accept balls in position or insist that conditions previous to foul be restored. Referee is sole judge in restoring balls to position.

Penalties: Penalties are paid by deducting points from the offending player's score.

If a player fouls and has no points to his credit, the fouls are charged against him and deducted from his score after he counts. On the running score, his record can show —1 or —2 and so on. If a player wins the game while his opponent, failing to score, has two penalties against him, the score would read 125 to —2. If a player has 15 points to his credit and loses a point through a penalty, his score is 14 until he legally counts in subsequent innings.

Loss of five points: If, in the referee's opinion, a player is unnecessarily delaying the game or is obviously employing dilatory or ungentlemanly methods to disturb or disconcert his opponent, or when it is obvious to the referee that a player, by the use of any of the above mentioned tactics, is establishing, from the spectator's point of view, a harmful impression of championship competition at the game of pocket billiards, the referee is vested with the authority to either penalize the player by deducting not more than five points from his score, or the referee may for repetition of offense or for any extreme offense forfeit the game to offending player's opponent.

Unnecessary delay: Delay of the game for more than one minute between shots may be considered just cause for imposition of the five-point penalty.

Referee should have a stop-watch to time delays on the part of a player who is obviously wasting time.

Safety play: Safety play is legal. The player may or may not declare his intention to play safe to the referee. If it is obvious to the referee that a player resorted to safety without declaring his intention, the referee announces "safety" after the balls stop rolling.

In attempting a safety, player must drive an object ball to a cushion, pocket an object ball, or cause the cue ball to strike a cushion after contacting object ball. Failure is a foul. Penalty: loss of one point.

Loss of 15 points: When a player has scratched, he loses

MOSCONI ON POCKET BILLIARDS

his inning, forfeits one point, and a notation that he has one scratch against him is posted on the score board in full view of the players and referee. The scratch is not in any way affected by opponent's play. Offending player must remove the scratch either by pocketing a ball at his next turn at the table, or by playing a legal safety. If he scratches during his next appearance at the table, with one scratch against him, he loses his inning, forfeits another point and "two scratches" against him are posted on the score board. Again the offending player may remove the scratches by pocketing a ball, or by playing a legal safety during his next inning; but if he scratches for a third time in succession, he loses one point for the third scratch, plus FIFTEEN points for the three successive scratches, and is required, with cue ball in hand, to break the balls as of the opening break shot. (In other words, players lose a total of 18 points for three successive scratches.) In making break shot after three successive scratches, rules for break shot apply. *(See* Requirements of Break, *above.)*

If, in the opinion of the referee, a player willfully moves the cue ball for safety play other than with the tip of the cue, or in any way willfully commits a foul, he shall forfeit 15 points, which are deducted from his score. Incoming player accepts balls in position.

Ball bouncing from pocket: If an object ball falls into a pocket and then rebounds on the table, it is not to be considered a pocketed ball. If the ball in question is the called ball, the player loses his inning. The ball remains in play where it comes to rest on the table.

Jumped balls: If the cue ball jumps off the table, it is a foul. Player loses inning and forfeits one point. A scratch is marked against him. Incoming player has cue ball in hand.

If the called object ball jumps the table, it is a miss and ends the player's inning. Retrieved object ball is spotted. If the player scores the called object ball and then, as the result of the stroke, causes another object ball to jump the table, the retrieved ball is spotted, the player is credited with the ball legally counted and continues play.

The lighting fixtures, when placed directly over the table, shall be considered part of the equipment. Should a ball leave the table, strike the lighting fixtures and then return to the table, it remains in play where it comes to rest. No penalty applies.

If a ball jumps the table, rides a rail, and then returns to the table, it remains in play where it comes to rest. It is not considered a jumped ball. No penalty applies.

If a ball leaves the table and comes to rest on a rail, without returning to the table bed, it is considered a jumped ball. Rules for jump balls apply, depending upon whether the ball is the cue ball or an object ball.

Jump shots: Jump shots may or may not be illegal, depending on the following:

1. If a player causes the cue ball to jump (rise from the bed of the table) accidentally, as the result of a legal stroke, or deliberately, by elevating the butt end of the cue and striking the cue ball in the center or above center, the jump is legal.
2. If, however, a player digs under the cue ball with the tip end of the cue, causing the ball to jump, the stroke is foul. Penalty: loss of one point.

Object ball within string: If a player has the cue ball in hand and all object balls on the table are within the head string (between the head string and the head of the table) the object ball closest to the string is spotted on the foot spot. If two object balls appear to be equidistant from the string, the lowest-numbered ball is placed on the foot spot. Player, with cue ball in hand, plays from any point of his choosing within the head string, shooting at the ball on the foot spot.

Cue ball in hand: The cue ball is in hand at the beginning of the game, also when forced off the table or pocketed, and when for any reason 15 balls are framed (except as superseded by the following "interference" rule). The cue ball remains in hand until the player drives it from within the head string to an object between the head string and the foot of the table.

Interference with racking of balls: Whenever by accident or design a player by one stroke legally pockets the 14th and 15th balls of a frame, he is entitled to both balls, the 15 object balls are reframed, and the player continues play from where the cue ball came to rest.

Interference with rack: If an unpocketed ball (the 15th ball of the frame) interferes with the racking of the 14 balls, the unpocketed ball is placed on the head spot.

If the cue ball and the unpocketed object ball interfere with the racking of the 14 balls, the 15 object balls are racked and the player has the cue ball in hand.

If the cue ball interferes with the racking of the 14 object balls, the following applies:

1. The cue ball is in hand if the break object ball (outside the rack) is not within the head string (between the head string and the head of the table).
2. If break ball is within the head string, the cue ball is placed on the head spot. (If the break ball rests on the head spot, the cue ball is placed on the center spot.)

In any event, as a result of interference with racking the 14 balls, the player has the option of shooting at break ball (providing it has not been racked) or any ball in the rack. If the player elects to shoot into the rack, he must drive an object ball to a cushion, or cause the cue ball to hit a cushion after contacting an object ball or pocket a ball. Failure is a foul. Penalty: loss of one point.

Outside interference: Ball accidentally or deliberately disturbed by a person other than the player at the table must be replaced as near as possible to its position before interference. Player continues his inning.

Stroke is complete: A counting stroke cannot be regarded as complete until all the balls on the table have come to a dead stop. This rule also applies to spinning balls. Player who shoots while the cue ball or an object ball is in motion or spinning is guilty of a foul. Penalty: loss of one point.

Time limit on protests: If a player, in the opinion of his opponent, is guilty of a foul, the opponent may ask for a ruling by the referee. Complaining player, however, must enter his protest before player allegedly making foul shoots again after foul. Complaints registered after a subsequent stroke cannot be honored.

Line-up Pocket Billiards

This game is played with 15 object balls, numbered from 1 to 15, and a cue ball. Object balls are racked on the foot spot, as in 14.1 continuous pocket billiards. (*See* Diagram 7.) Starting player has cue ball in hand. It is a call shot game, players being required to call the ball and the pocket.

Each ball legally pocketed gives the scorer credit for one point. All balls pocketed on a legally called shot count, the player getting one point for each ball.

Game is an agreed upon number of points — it can be 25, 50, 100, or whatever score agreed upon.

Start of play: Rotation of play can be determined by lag or lot. Winner of lag has option of breaking or assigning break to his opponent.

Starting player must pocket a called ball in the rack or drive two object balls to a cushion. Failure to do so is a foul. Offending player forfeits two points. Opponent can require that offender break again until he complies with the break-shot requirements. Player loses two points for each successive failure.

Subsequent play: After the legal break shot, if starting player has not scored, incoming player accepts balls in position. He must call his shots — ball and pocket — on all strokes. Player continues until he misses. At the conclusion of his inning, he records his points, and all balls he scored are spotted on the long string line. *(See* Diagram 5.) *(See* spotting balls, Rotation.)

If player scores all 15 balls, they are spotted on the string line and he continues play, shooting cue ball from where it came to rest after preceding stroke.

Penalties: When a player fouls, he is penalized one point. Only one penalty is imposed, however, if the player fouls more than once on the same stroke.

General rules: The rules for 14.1 continuous pocket billiards apply to line-up pocket billiards. Balls scored on foul strokes do not count. Penalties are paid out of the player's score. If he has no points at time of foul, he owes a point, which is deducted after he scores.

APPENDIX C

World Pocket Billiard Champions and Records*

Champions

Cyrille Dion.......1878-80
Gottlieb Wahlstrom...1881
Albert Frey........1882-83
J. L. Malone.........1884
Albert Frey........1886-87
P. L. Malone
   (forfeit) 1887
Alfredo DeOro.....1887-88
Frank Powers........1888
Albert Frey 1889
Alfredo DeOro 1889
H. Manning 1890
Frank Powers
   (forfeit) 1891
Alfredo DeOro 1892-94
Wm. Clearwater 1895
Alfredo DeOro 1895
Frank Stewart
   (forfeit) 1896
Grant Eby 1897
Jerome Keogh 1897
Wm. Clearwater 1898
Jerome Keogh 1898
Alfredo DeOro ...1899-1900
Frank Sherman 1901
Alfredo DeOro 1901
Wm. Clearwater 1902

Grant Eby 1902
Alfredo DeOro 1903
Alfredo DeOro 1904
Jerome Keogh
   (forfeit) 1905
Alfredo DeOro 1905
Thos. Hueston
   (forfeit) 1905
Thos. Hueston 1906
John Horgan 1906
Jerome Keogh 1906
Thos. Hueston 1907
Thos. Hueston 1908
Frank Sherman 1908
Alfredo DeOro 1908
Chas. Weston 1909
John Kling 1909
Thos. Hueston 1910
Jerome Keogh 1910
Alfredo DeOro 1910-12
R. J. Ralph 1912
Alfredo DeOro 1913
Bennie Allen 1913-15
John Layton 1916
Frank Taberski 1916-18
Ralph Greenleaf ...1919-24
Frank Taberski 1925

---

*Reprinted by permission from *The Official Billiard Rule Book*.

Ralph Greenleaf 1926	Ralph Greenleaf 1937
Erwin Rudolph 1926	James Caras 1938
Thos. Hueston 1926	James Caras 1939
Frank Taberski 1927	Andrew Ponzi* 1940
Ralph Greenleaf ...1927-28	Willie Mosconi* 1941
Frank Taberski 1928	Erwin Rudolph† 1941
Ralph Greenleaf 1929	Irving Crane‡ 1942
Frank Taberski 1929	Willie Mosconi‡ ...1942-43
Erwin Rudolph 1930	Andrew Ponzi‡ 1943
Ralph Greenleaf ...1930-32	Willie Mosconi‡..1944-45-46
Erwin Rudolph 1933-34	Irving Crane† 1946-47
Andrew Ponzi 1935	Willie Mosconi‡ ...1947-48
James Caras 1936	James Caras 1949
	Willie Mosconi 1950-58

* League Play.   † Tournament.   ‡ Match.

Records — 14.1 Pocket Billiards

1929 — Ralph Greenleaf — Tourn.
   5′ x 10′ table ....High run 126
1929 — Ralph Greenleaf — Tourn.
   High single average, 5′ x 10′ table 63
1929 — Ralph Greenleaf — Tourn.
   High Individual grand average, 5′ x 10′ table 11.02
1929 — Best Game — Ralph Greenleaf, 2 innings,
   5′ x 10′ table
1939 — Andrew Ponzi (League play)........High run 127
1941 — Best Game — Willie Mosconi,
   5′ x 10′ table ....2 innings
1945 — Willie Mosconi (Exh. high run) 527
1945 — Willie Mosconi (Match-Single Game) High run 127
1946 — James Caras (Match-Single Game)....High run 127
1947 — Willie Mosconi — Grand Average (2,000 pts.)..15.85
1948 — Willie Mosconi — Grand Average (1,350 pts.) ..19
1955 — Joe Procita — Match ....High run 182
1956 — Best Game — Tourn. — Willie Mosconi..1 inning
1956 — High Run —Tourn. — Willie Mosconi 150